# Edexcel

# Functional Skills
# English

**Written by** Eileen Sagar and Keith Washington

**Consultants:** Jen Greatrex and Bill Kaill

## Level 2

# Teacher Guide

A PEARSON COMPANY

Heinemann is an imprint of Pearson Education Limited,
a company incorporated in England and Wales, having its
registered office at Edinburgh Gate, Harlow, Essex, CM20 2JE.
Registered company number: 872828

www.pearsonschoolsandfecolleges.co.uk

Heinemann is a registered trademark of Pearson Education Limited

Text © Pearson Education Limited, 2010

First published 2010

12 11 10
10 9 8 7 6 5 4 3 2 1

**British Library Cataloguing in Publication Data**
A catalogue record for this book is available from the British
Library.

ISBN 978 1 846 907 14 2

Produced by Pearson Education Ltd, 2010
Designed and produced by Kamae Design, Oxford
Original illustrations © Pearson Education, 2010
Cover design by Pete Stratton
Cover photo/illustration © Shutterstock Images
Printed in the UK by Ashford Colour Press

**Acknowledgements**
The author and publisher would like to thank the following
individuals and organisations for permission to reproduce
copyright material:

Article "Motorists back etiquette section for driving test" by John
Bingham, from The Telegraph. Reproduced with permission of the
Telegraph Media Group; Extract from "Satellite navigation". Article
produced by the Department for Transport; Extract from "Gift ideas
to avoid". Article produced by Big Fat Balloons; Extract from "Gifts
– Your Rights". Article produced by Leicestershire County Council
Trading Standards Service. Reproduced with permission; Paintball
Pass/Horse Drawn Carriage Country Pub Run/Gorge walking
experience adverts by intotheblue.co.uk.

Every effort has been made to contact copyright holders of
material reproduced in this book. Any omissions will be rectified in
subsequent printings if notice is given to the publishers.

Thanks to the staff and students at Holyhead School, Handsworth
for their invaluable help with research and exemplar students' work.

# Contents

# Introduction

The Functional Skills English qualification is designed to give candidates the skills to operate confidently, effectively and independently in education, work and everyday life. This has been created in response to employers' perceptions that students are not achieving a sufficiently firm grounding in the basics.

## About this Teacher Guide

All materials in this Teacher Guide will help you with the planning, delivery and assessment preparation of Functional Skills English. All pages are provided in both print and CD form, so that you may print off the resources you require, and if you wish adapt them to your own requirements.

## Schemes of work

This Teacher Guide provides schemes of work for delivering the three elements of Functional Skills English – Reading, Speaking, Listening and Communication and Writing – at Level 2, using the Level 2 student book. On pages 1 to 5 of this guide you will find summary schemes of work for each of the three elements, based on the content in the student book. The schemes of work are expanded in the lesson plans on pages 20 to 47.

## Lesson plans and approaches to teaching

All lessons in the student book are supported by lesson plans. These give clear guidance on:

- the aims and learning objectives for the lesson
- how to introduce the lesson in a starter activity
- working through the teaching text and activities in the student book effectively
- how to draw the lesson together in a plenary
- ideas for homework.

All the activities in the lesson plans can be approached via a range of methods – individual work, pairs, small groups, pairs with an observer who feeds back, or whole class with white board or posters. You should use a variety of these approaches, deciding which is most appropriate for specific classes/lessons.

The lesson plans also offer sample student answers to activities in the student book where appropriate, giving you a ready-to-use benchmark for what to expect from your students. Each section of lesson plans is introduced by an overview of how to approach teaching, with teaching ideas and guidance related to the lessons.

The length of lessons will vary according to the interests and abilities of your students. You may wish to tailor the materials as you use them, by using the files on the CD.

## Integrating with the Key Stage 3 curriculum or with GCSE

Functional Skills English can be taught during KS3 or alongside GCSE. Customisable matching grids for both are provided on pages 7 to 14 to assist with your planning.

## Assessment preparation and practice

Clear guidance on how students will be assessed is provided on pages 49 to 51. This guidance is also provided direct to the student in appropriate language within the student book (pages 110 to 115), and supplemented with *Top tips* for success.

In addition, each section in the student book ends with a *Test zone*. Here students are given examples of the kinds of questions and tasks they will encounter in their assessments, helpfully annotated by the examiner to draw attention to what is required. Share these sections with students and have them complete the questions, drawing on the examiner's supporting comments, to embed understanding of how they will be assessed. Use the sample answers at pass and fail, the accompanying summaries from the examiner and the self assessment features in the student book to further develop their understanding. Draw attention to the tips from the examiner, provided for all lessons, which direct students to both common errors and strategies for working effectively.

On pages 52 to 73 of this guide you will find reproduced the full text of the sample assessment materials issued by Edexcel. Use these to give your students a full assessment practice. Pages 74 to 98 offer examples of students' responses to the sample assessment materials, helping you to demonstrate to students what represents a fail or a pass answer. Use the examiner's commentary to expand upon what is required to gain marks.

Further complete practice assessments are provided at the end of the student book and on pages 99 to 119 of this guide.

# Reading

## Introduction to the scheme of work for Reading

Functional English Level 2 Reading helps students to develop a range of skills for reading, understanding and comparing texts.

*The Level 2 skill standard for reading: select, read, understand and compare texts and use them to gather information, ideas, arguments and opinions.* These skills help students to:

- select and use different types of texts to obtain and utilise relevant information

- read and summarise succinctly information/ideas from different sources
- identify the purposes of texts and comment on how meaning is conveyed
- detect points of view, implicit meaning and/or bias
- analyse texts in response to audience needs and consider suitable responses.

| Lesson | Aim | Learning objective | Activities | Resources |
|---|---|---|---|---|
| **1 Reading different kinds of texts** | Learning to choose and use varied types of text for information. | Choose and use different texts to find relevant information. | Students review different text features and how they can be used to understand a text and find information. They then practise finding specific information by navigating the text using the organisational features. | Student book pages 8–11 |
| **2 Skimming, scanning and close reading** | Reading to suit different purposes: skimming, scanning and close reading of texts. | Use different reading skills to find relevant information. | Students use different styles of reading to answer questions that relate to the skills they are using. | Student book pages 12–13 |
| **3 Finding main ideas and details** | Read and summarise succinctly and identify the purpose of texts. | Find and use main ideas and details in texts. | Students read sample texts and try to find main ideas or points in them. | Student book pages 14–15. Teacher-researched texts for practising the skills. |
| **4 Comparing texts** | Read and summarise succinctly information/ideas from different sources. | Compare texts. Choose and use different texts to find relevant information. | Students compare two texts identifying what about them is true/false, as well as what about them is the same and what is different about them. Students learn to compare and contrast. | Student book pages 16–17. Optional, additional teacher-researched texts for practising the skills. |
| **5 Selecting relevant information from more than one text** | Select and use different types of text, and summarise succinctly information/ideas from different sources. | Choose and use different texts to find relevant information. | Students read various kinds of text types and draw out relevant information from them, in order to answer questions related to the texts and to make decisions of judgement based on the information extracted from the texts. | Student book pages 18–19 |
| **6 Understanding tables** | The use of tables and finding information in them. | Use tables to find relevant information. | Students are presented with various table formats from which they find information to suit a specific purpose/ scenario. | Student book pages 20–21. Real-life samples of tables (pricelists, timetables, charts, etc). |

| | | | | Student book pages |
|---|---|---|---|---|
| **7 Summarising information and ideas** | Read and summarise information/ideas from different sources. | Read and briefly summarise information and ideas from different texts. | Students read various types of texts and summarise the main points/ideas/opinions presented. | Student book pages 22–23 |
| **8 Understanding the purpose of a text** | Identify the purpose of texts (and comment on how meaning is conveyed). | Work out and understand the purpose of a text. | Students are presented with various types of text, from which they identify the main purpose of a text (e.g. to inform, to sell, to advise and so on). | Student book pages 24–25 |
| **9 How writers communicate meaning** | Understanding how writers communicate meaning and recognising the meaning. | Comment on how a writer communicates the meaning of a text. | Students note down the purposes of texts used, as they have learned in previous lessons. Then they find features, such as heading, caption, bullet points, list, image(s) and interpret their meaning in relation to the reader and audience. | Student book page 26–27 Flip chart/Interactive white board Optional, additional teacher-researched texts for practising the skills. |
| **10 Understanding implied meanings** | Detect point of view, implicit meaning and/ or bias. | Understand meanings that are hinted at or suggested. Be able to identify facts and opinions. | Students read different types of texts and identify points of view, bias and/or implicit meaning in them. They also practise distinguishing fact(s) and opinion(s). | Student book pages 28–29 |
| **11 Identifying points of view and bias** | Detect points of view and bias. | Recognise points of view and bias, understand how these can affect meaning. | Students detect points of view and bias, and their effect on meaning through reading sample texts. From them they pick out words and phrases that reveal points of view. | Student book pages 30–31 |
| **12 Consider suitable responses to texts** | Analyse texts in relation to audience needs and consider suitable responses. | Consider texts in terms of the writer's purpose and the readers' needs. Work out what a suitable response to a text is. | Students identify texts' purpose, audience, the given information, words and phrases as well as other factors such as if the texts are trustworthy or reliable, finally deciding on a sensible response to a text. | Student book pages 32–33 |

# Speaking, listening and communication

## Introduction to the scheme of work for Speaking, Listening and Communication

Functional English Level 2 Speaking, Listening and Communication helps students to develop their skills in contributing to discussions and making effective presentations.

*Level 2 skill standard for speaking, listening and communication: make a range of contributions to discussions in a range of contexts, including those that are unfamiliar, and make effective presentations.* These skills help students to:

- consider complex information and give a relevant, cogent response in appropriate language
- present information and ideas clearly and persuasively to others
- adapt contributions to suit audience, purpose and situation
- make significant contributions to discussions, taking a range of roles and helping to move discussion forward.

| Lesson | Aim | Learning objective | Activities | Resources |
|---|---|---|---|---|
| 1 Taking part in discussions | Make significant contributions to discussions, taking a range of roles and move discussion forward. | Plan and prepare a group discussion, and take a range of roles in a formal discussion. | Students practise group discussion situations in varied scenarios, based on sample texts in the student book. | Student book pages 48–51 |
| 2 Making effective presentations | Planning and preparing a presentation and interaction with the audience. | Plan, prepare and give a well organised presentation, tailored to your audience; listen carefully and respond to questions from your audience. | Students practise making a presentation, based on details given. They plan the presentation and use a table structure to consider what the presentation is about, as well as what the audience may want to know. Students plan their points and arguments, consider the correct language to use, and learn to use visual aids, where appropriate. | Student book pages 52–55 |

# Writing

## Introduction to the scheme of work for Writing

Functional English Level 2 Writing develops students' writing skills in a range of texts and contexts.

*Level 2 skill standard for writing: write a range of texts, including extended written documents, communicating information, ideas and opinions effectively and persuasively.* These skills help students to:

- present information/ideas concisely, logically and persuasively
- present information on complex subjects clearly and concisely
- use a range of writing styles for different purposes

- use a range of sentence structures, including complex sentences and paragraphs to organise written communication effectively
- punctuate written text using commas, apostrophes and inverted commas accurately
- ensure written work is fit for purpose and audience, with accurate spelling and grammar that support clear meaning in a range of text types.

| Lesson | Aim | Learning objective | Activities | Resources |
|---|---|---|---|---|
| 1 Thinking about your audience | Ensure written work is fit for purpose and audience. | Suit the content and style of your writing to your audience. | Students are presented with scenarios, for which they identify the prospective audience(s) and then they ensure their writing is fit for purpose. | Student book pages 64–65 |
| 2 Writing to suit a purpose | Understanding writing form and fitting it for purpose. | Suit your content and style to the purpose of your writing. | Students learn to write a letter, an article, an email and generally suit those for the purpose, presenting ideas succinctly and clearly. | Student book pages 66–67<br><br>Flip chart |
| 3 Understanding form | Recognising different styles of writing, for different purposes, and with a reference to being fit for purpose. | Choose the right form for your writing, and include the features of different forms in your writing. | Students study various types of texts (e.g. a report, briefing paper, magazine article and letter, etc.) and note down the form and what features each type of text typically contain. | Student book pages 68–73 |
| 4 Understanding style | Understanding various styles of writing and learning to suit own writing to purpose. | Write in a style that is suited to your purpose and audience. | Students work out the audience, purpose, etc. within a scenario, writing letters, emails and articles to fit that purpose. | Student book pages 74–75 |
| 5 Writing formal letters | Writing formal letters using form, style and paragraphs effectively. | Write a well organised, formal letter and email, use paragraphs effectively, and ensure meaning is clear by using connectives effectively. | Students study a letter, noting down what it consists of. Then they write a letter in the same vein, structuring and planning it by using flowcharts and using salutations, paragraphing and persuasive techniques, accurately and where appropriate. | Student book pages 76–81<br><br>Flip chart |

| Lesson | Aim | Learning objective | Activities | Resources |
|---|---|---|---|---|
| 6 Planning and organising your writing | Learning to effectively plan and organise ideas, presenting complex information clearly. | Plan and organise your ideas, present complex information clearly, making meaning clear by using subject and verb agreement accurately. | Students are asked to write a 500 word magazine article. Prior to this they practise planning the writing with flow charts and spider diagrams, making a note of purpose and audience. | Student book pages 82–85 |
| 7 Writing a briefing paper | Researching and understanding the basic structure and purpose of a briefing paper. Using apostrophes correctly. | Research and write a briefing paper, and make meaning clear by using apostrophes correctly. | Students study a sample briefing paper, noting its features and make conclusions from it. Then, they create one, using correct form and various styles of delivering the information (e.g. normal text, headings, bullet points, numbered lists, etc.), and remembering the correct use of apostrophes. | Student book pages 86–89 |
| 8 Making a convincing argument | Effectively building clear arguments and backing up ideas/opinions with evidence. | Plan how to back up your ideas with evidence, build your argument and ensure your meaning is clear by using inverted commas correctly. | Students write a magazine article arguing for or against an idea. They decide on purpose and audience, plan carefully and write a PEEL paragraph. They then answer some questions on inverted commas. | Student book pages 90–93 |
| 9 Writing a report | Writing clear reports, concise in meaning and accurate, with correct spelling and grammar. | Write a report; use verbs in correct tenses so that meaning is clear; ensure meaning is clear by improving your spelling; check your work to ensure it is clear and accurate. | Students discuss the purpose of reports, pick out features of one, then write a first draft of their own. They then practice using verbs in the current tense, make up rules for using homophones, and check their work to ensure it is clear and accurate. | Student book pages 94–99 |

# KS3 matching grids

Functional Skills English is taught through the English programmes of study. There are important distinctions that need to be observed, however, such as the key concept of competence. Competence is defined as *being clear and coherent in spoken and written communication.*

## Reading

The successful student will be expected to move beyond the Level 1 requirement to *understand texts in detail.* There must be evidence of the ability to select and use different types of texts and to synthesise information. Understanding of possible intended purpose of texts and how meaning is conveyed are also essential Level 2 skills.

Linked to this is the ability to distinguish between fact and opinion as identified in the programme of study, and as described in the coverage and range *to detect point of view, implicit meaning and/or bias.* Over the past two decades, there has been recognition that there is a need for students to read and understand texts in different forms and written for different purposes, whilst still retaining study of literary texts, drawn from different genre, cultures and times. Essentially, reading and the assessment of reading in Functional Skills English makes the focus texts that are grounded in real-life contexts and responses to these texts will reflect situations in life, rather than an empathetic response.

The focus in reading is in that sense, narrow, and responds to a need in society for its members to make informed judgements and frame appropriate responses within realistic contexts. You will notice that texts used for assessment of Functional Skills English in reading are authentic, drawn from a range of documents such as leaflets, articles, guidance documents, letters and websites, to name a few.

## Speaking, listening and communication

At Level 1, students show that they are functional in informal and formal discussions and exchanges. At Level 2, students also need to be functional in making effective presentations and speaking, listening and communicating in a wide range of contexts including those that are unfamiliar.

Competence in the programmes of study also means *being adaptable in a widening range of familiar and unfamiliar contexts* and this extends beyond the learning environment. Additionally, communicating either formally or informally will be decided through informed choices. Using speaking and listening for dramatic effect or for literary presentations has its place in the KS3 English

programmes of study, but not in preparing your students to be functional. The areas of the programmes of study that reflect functional English have been identified and mapped to the skill standard and coverage and range.

## Writing

Writing needs to reflect the types of writing that will be necessary in the world of work and society in general. Section 2.3 of the KS3 programmes of study makes composition its focus. This refers to many features that are recognisably functional. The references to aspects linked with creative responses have been removed for the purposes of this guidance. While these continue to be an essential part of the English curriculum, they are not part of the skills standard or the coverage and range.

As is the case in the coverage and range, the composition sections of the programmes of study place emphasis on clarity, adapting writing for audience and purpose, using a range of sentence structures and ensuring that the writing is fit for purpose. Significant importance is given to technical accuracy in the programmes of study. This is also evident in the standards. As is the case with the other two components, writing tasks must be contextualised and rooted in 'authentic' real-life situations. It is essential that students answer each task as closely as possible. If asked to write a formal letter, it is expected that they are able to present their response in the appropriate layout and using the appropriate tone/register, for example.

Section 4.3 of the programmes of study expands on writing for contexts and purposes beyond the classroom. To be functional in Level 2 Writing, the students must use the appropriate form and demonstrate this ability more than once, usually with a different form, audience and purpose. In the programmes of study forms of writing that would be potentially functional include articles, letters, reports and commentaries.

The student has to pass each component in order to be awarded a Functional Skills English level, as this is not a compensatory model of assessment. The mapping is designed to illustrate how specified aspects of the programmes of study can be mapped to the coverage and range in Functional Skills English. It is essential to deliver a teaching programme that targets functional skills in English as part of the curriculum. A very important message to emerge from this qualification in its pilot stage is that the more successful learners are those who have been carefully prepared for what is a highly specified qualification.

# Reading

| Functional Skills | SB pages | 6–45 |
|---|---|---|
| | Level | 2 |
| | Skill standard | Select, read, understand and compare texts, and use them to gather information, ideas, arguments and opinions. |
| | Coverage and range | • Select and use different types of texts to obtain and utilise relevant information.<br>• Read and summarise succinctly information/ideas from different sources.<br>• Identify the purposes of texts and comment on how effectively meaning is conveyed.<br>• Detect point of view, implicit meaning and/or bias.<br>• Analyse texts in relation to audience needs and consider suitable response.<br>*(in three or more texts)* |

**Links to KS3 Programme of Study**

**Key processes include:**

- Extract and interpret information, events, main points and ideas from texts.
- Infer and deduce meaning.
- Assess the usefulness of texts.
- Sift the relevant from the irrelevant.
- Distinguish between fact and opinion.

**Key concepts include:**

- Reading and understanding a range of texts.

**Range and content includes:**

- The range of non-fiction and non-literary texts studied should include: form, such as journalism, travel writing, essays, reportage, literary non-fiction and multi-modal texts including film; purposes, such as to instruct, inform, explain, describe, analyse, review, discuss and persuade.

# Speaking, listening and communication

<table>
<tr><td rowspan="5">**Functional Skills**</td><td>**SB pages**</td><td>46–69</td></tr>
<tr><td>**Level**</td><td>2</td></tr>
<tr><td>**Skill standard**</td><td>Make a range of contributions to discussions in a range of contexts, including those that are unfamiliar, and make effective presentations.</td></tr>
<tr><td>**Coverage and range**</td><td>
• Consider complex information and give a relevant, cogent response in appropriate language.<br>
• Present information and ideas clearly and persuasively to others.<br>
• Adapt contributions to suit audience, purpose and situation.<br>
• Make significant contributions to discussions, taking a range of roles and helping to move discussion forward.</td></tr>
<tr><td colspan="2">

**Key processes include:**

• Make relevant contributions in groups, responding appropriately to others.
• Adapt talk for a range of purposes and audiences.
• Make different kinds of contributions.
• Present information/points of view clearly and in appropriate language in formal and informal exchanges, as well as discussions.

**Range and content includes:**

• The range of speaking and listening activities should include prepared formal presentations and debates.
• The range of purposes for speaking and listening should include expressing ideas and opinions.</td></tr>
</table>

(Left side label for bottom row: **Links to KS3 Programme of Study**)

# Writing

| | | |
|---|---|---|
| **Functional Skills** | **SB pages** | 60–101 |
| | **Level** | 2 |
| | **Skill standard** | Write a range of texts, including extended written documents, communicating information, ideas and opinions, effectively and persuasively. |
| | **Coverage and range** | • Present information/ideas concisely, logically and persuasively.<br>• Present information on complex subjects concisely and clearly.<br>• Use a range of writing styles for different purposes.<br>• Use a range of sentence structures, including complex sentences and paragraphs to organise written communication effectively.<br>• Punctuate accurately using commas, apostrophes and inverted commas.<br>• Ensure written work is fit for purpose and audience, with accurate spelling and grammar that support clear meaning.<br>*(in a range of text types)* |

**Links to KS3 Programme of Study**

**Key processes include:**

- Write clearly and coherently, including an appropriate level of detail.
- Structure their writing to support the purpose for the task and organise meaning.
- Adapt style and language appropriately for a range of forms, purposes and readers.
- Use grammar accurately in a variety of sentence types, including subject-verb agreement and correct and consistent use of tense.
- Use planning, drafting, editing, proof reading and self evaluation to shape and craft their writing for maximum effect.

**Range and content includes:**

- The forms for such writing should be drawn from different kinds of stories, poems, play-scripts, autobiographies, screenplays, diaries, minutes, accounts, information leaflets, plans, summaries, brochures, advertisements, editorials, articles and letters conveying opinions, campaign literature, polemics, reviews, commentaries, articles, essays and reports.

# GCSE matching grids

The National Curriculum English programmes of study include functional English. 'In studying English, students develop skills in speaking, listening, reading and writing that they will need to participate in society and employment.' This statement, taken from 'The importance of English', in the programme of study for KS4 makes a clear link with functionality, and one of the key concepts identified and exemplified is competence. The five areas identified are entirely functional in their focus. Functional Skills English can be co-taught with GCSE English and English Language and this is demonstrated in the mapping of the three Functional Skills English components to the Edexcel English/English Language GCSE Units 1 and 3.

The student has to pass each component (Reading; Speaking: Listening and Communication; and Writing) in order to be awarded Level 2 in Functional Skills English. The mapping is designed to illustrate how specified aspects of the programme of study can be mapped to the coverage and range in Functional Skills English. It is essential to deliver a teaching programme that targets functional skills in English as part of the curriculum.

## Reading

In GCSE English and English Language, students are required to respond to a range of literary and non-literary texts. The key difference between this and Functional Skills English is in the need to respond to literary texts in GCSE. The similarities in the assessment requirements demonstrate that there is a significant overlap in terms of responding to non-literary texts and it is this overlap that makes co-teaching viable and enables an integrated approach to teaching.

Level 2 requires students to select, read, understand and compare texts, using them to gather information, ideas, arguments and opinions. They need to demonstrate the ability to select and use different types of texts, read and summarise succinctly, identify purpose and how meaning is conveyed, detect point of view, implicit meaning/bias and analyse texts in relation to audience needs and consider suitable responses. The GCSE criteria, drawn from the programme of study, requires that the students demonstrate the ability to read and understand texts, select material appropriate to purpose, collate from different sources, making comparisons and cross-references as appropriate. They should also be able to explain and evaluate how writers use linguistic, grammatical features to achieve effects and engage and influence the reader. The mapping shows that this is assessed in Functional Skills Reading too.

There is continuing recognition of the need for students to read and understand texts in different forms and written for different purposes, whilst still retaining study of literary texts, drawn from different genre, cultures and times. Essentially, texts in Functional Skills Reading assessments are grounded in real-life contexts and responses need to be appropriately framed. You will notice that texts used for assessment of Functional Skills are drawn from a range of documents we encounter in real life, such as leaflets, articles, guidance documents, letters and web pages, to name a few. Such texts are also evident in GCSE and require students to make appropriate responses to them. The programme of study identifies the need for students to understand the origin and purpose of texts coming from a range of sources, including websites.

## Speaking, listening and communication

In Functional Skills English, students need to be competent in both familiar and unfamiliar contexts. In Level 2 there are two areas for assessment: discussion and presentation. Students are required to consider complex information and make relevant responses using appropriate language. They need to demonstrate the ability to present information and ideas clearly and persuasively, adapt contributions to suit audience, purpose and situation and make significant contributions to discussions, adopting a range of roles to move the discussion forward. These skils are identified in 2.1 of the programme of study, where students need to demonstrate the ability to listen to complex information, make cogent responses, present information clearly, use a range of strategies and sustain discussion in different contexts. The GCSE subject criteria requires the candidate to communicate purposefully, structure and sustain talk, adapting it to different situations and audiences, use standard English and a variety of techniques as appropriate, and listen and respond to speakers' ideas and perspectives.

The main difference between GCSE and Functional Skills is in the creating and sustaining roles. In GCSE, this will also include creating a dramatic role involving the imagination. In Functional Skills English, this refers to the types of roles that are grounded in real-life contexts such as chairing a discussion or interviewing someone. It is possible to assess any dramatic elements separately for GCSE and co-teach to prepare students for assessments in both qualifications. The overlap with GCSE English is in discussion and communication. It would be logical to assess discussion and presentation for co-teaching Functional Skills English and GCSE and separately assess any imaginative role play such as undertaking a role drawn from a literary text.

## Writing

Similarly, in the area of writing, contexts must be grounded in reality and the writing needs to reflect the types of writing that will be necessary in the world of work and society in general. This refers to features that are recognisably functional. The GCSE criteria require that candidates write to communicate clearly, effectively and imaginatively, using and adapting forms and selecting vocabulary appropriately to task and purpose in ways that engage the reader. Candidates must also organise information and ideas into structured and sequenced sentences, paragraphs and whole texts, using a variety of linguistic and structural features to support overall coherence. They will need to demonstrate the ability to use a range of sentence structures for clarity, purpose and effect, with accurate punctuation and spelling. The references to aspects of writing linked with creative responses have been removed for the purposes of this guidance. While these continue to be an essential part of the English curriculum, they are not part of the skills standard and the coverage and range in the 'Functional Skills Criteria for English' document.

As is the case in the coverage and range, the composition section of the programme of study places emphasis on fluent writing, presenting information on complex subjects, using a range of ways to structure whole texts, a wide range of persuasive techniques and a wide variety of sentence structures. Significant importance is given to technical accuracy. This is also evident in the standards, where 40-45% of the assessment concerns accuracy. As is the case with the other two components, writing tasks must be contextualised and rooted in 'authentic' real-life situations. To be functional in Level 2 writing, students must demonstrate the ability to write according to audience and purpose, using the appropriate form more than once. In the programme of study forms of writing that would be potentially functional include articles, letters, reports and commentaries. (See 3.3 for the full range.)

# Reading

| SB pages | Level | Skill standard | Coverage and range | Assessment Objective | Content | Links to Edexcel English/ English Language GCSE Unit 1 |
| --- | --- | --- | --- | --- | --- | --- |
| | | | | | | Grade description |
| 6–45 | 2 | Compare, select, read and understand texts, and use them to gather information, ideas, arguments and opinions. | • Select and use different types of texts to obtain and utilise relevant information.<br>• Read and summarise succinctly information/ideas from different sources.<br>• Identify the purposes of texts and comment on how effectively meaning is conveyed.<br>• Detect point of view, implicit meaning and/or bias.<br>• Analyse texts in relation to audience needs and consider suitable response.<br>*(in three or more texts)* | (i) Read and understand, selecting material appropriate to purpose, collating from different sources and making comparisons and cross-references as appropriate.<br><br>(ii) Develop and sustain interpretations of writers' ideas and perspectives, referring closely to the development of narrative, argument, explanation or analysis.<br><br>(iii) Explain and evaluate how writers use linguistic, grammatical, structural and presentational features to achieve effects and engage the reader, supporting their comments with detailed textual references. | • Understand how meaning is constructed through words, sentences and whole texts, recognising and responding to the effects of language variation.<br>• Evaluate the ways in which texts may be interpreted differently according to the perspective of the reader. | **F**<br>Candidates describe the main ideas, themes or argument in a range of texts, and refer to specific aspects or details when justifying their views. They make simple comparisons and cross-references that show some awareness of how texts achieve their effects through writers' use of linguistic, grammatical, structural and presentational devices.<br><br>**C**<br>Candidates understand and demonstrate how meaning and information are conveyed in a range of texts. They make personal and critical responses, referring to specific aspects of language, grammar, structure and presentational devices to justify their views. They successfully compare and cross-reference aspects of texts and explain convincingly how they may vary in purpose and how they achieve different effects. |

| Functional Skills | | | | | Links to Edexcel English/ English Language GCSE Unit 3 |
|---|---|---|---|---|---|
| SB pages | Level | Skill standard | Coverage and range | Assessment Objective | Content | Grade description |
| 46–69 | 2 | Make a range of contributions to discussions in a range of contexts, including those that are unfamiliar, and make effective presentations. | • Consider complex information and give a relevant, cogent response in appropriate language.<br>• Present information and ideas clearly and persuasively to others.<br>• Adapt contributions in discussions to suit audience, purpose and situation.<br>• Make significant contributions to discussions, taking a range of roles and helping to move discussion forward to reach a decision. | (i) Communicate clearly and purposefully; structure and sustain talk, adapting it to different situations and audiences; use standard English and a variety of techniques as appropriate.<br>(ii) Listen and respond to speakers' ideas, perspectives and how they construct and express their meanings.<br>(iii) Interact with others, shaping meanings through suggestions, comments and questions and drawing ideas together.<br>(iv) Create and sustain different roles. | • Present and listen to information and ideas.<br>• Respond to the questions and views of others, adapting talk appropriately to context and audience.<br>• Make a range of effective contributions, using creative approaches to exploring questions, solving problems and developing ideas.<br>• Reflect and comment critically on their own and others' uses of language<br>• Participate in a range of contexts, including real-life uses of talk and audiences beyond the classroom. | **F**<br>Candidates talk confidently in familiar situations, showing some awareness of purpose and listeners' needs. They convey information, develop ideas and describe feelings clearly, using the main features of standard English as appropriate. They listen with concentration and make relevant responses to others' ideas and opinions. In formal and creative activities, they attempt to meet the demands of different roles.<br><br>**C**<br>Candidates adapt their talk to the demands of different situations and contexts. They recognise when standard English is required and use it confidently. They use different sentence structures and select vocabulary so that information, ideas and feelings are communicated clearly and the listener's interest is engaged. Through careful listening and by developing their own and others' ideas, they make significant contributions to discussion and participate effectively in creative activities. |

# Writing

| Functional Skills | | | | | Links to Edexcel English/ English Language GCSE Unit 1 | |
|---|---|---|---|---|---|---|
| **SB pages** | **Level** | **Skill standard** | **Coverage and range** | **Assessment Objective** | **Content** | **Grade description** |
| **60–101** | 2 | Write a range of texts, including extended written documents, communicating information, ideas and opinions, effectively and persuasively. | • Present information/ ideas concisely, logically and persuasively.<br>• Present information on complex subjects concisely and clearly.<br>• Use a range of writing styles for different purposes.<br>• Use a range of sentence structures, including complex sentences and paragraphs to organise written communication effectively.<br>• Punctuate accurately using commas, apostrophes and inverted commas.<br>• Ensure written work is fit for purpose and audience, with accurate spelling and grammar that support clear meaning.<br>*(in three or more texts)* | (i) Communicate clearly, effectively and imaginatively, using and adapting forms as well as selecting vocabulary appropriately to task and purpose in ways which engage the reader.<br>(ii) Organise information and ideas into well structured and sequenced sentences, paragraphs and whole texts, using a variety of linguistic and structural features to support cohesion and overall coherence.<br>(iii) Use a range of sentence structures for clarity, purpose and effect, with accurate punctuation and spelling. | • Write accurately and fluently, choosing content and adapting style and language to a wide range of forms, media, contexts, audiences and purposes. | **F**<br>Candidates' writing shows some adaptation of form and style for different tasks and purposes. It communicates simply and clearly with the reader. Sentences sequence events or ideas logically; vocabulary is sometimes chosen for variety and interest. Paragraphing is straightforward but effective; the structure of sentences, including some that are complex, is usually correct. Spelling and basic punctuation are mostly accurate.<br>**C**<br>Candidates' writing shows successful adaptation of form and style to different tasks and for various purposes. They use a range of sentence structures and varied vocabulary to create different effects and engage the reader's interest. Paragraphing is used effectively to make the sequence of events or development of ideas coherent and clear to the reader. Sentence structures are varied; punctuation and spelling are accurate and sometimes bold. |

# Skills checklist – Reading

This self-assessment tool is designed so that your students can use it to help them identify areas of strength and areas that need development. It is adapted from the criteria, but broken down into smaller sections so that your students can rate specific aspects of their performances in each of the three components. This will help them to be discerning in their identification of areas needing improvement. You might want to introduce each of the components alongside the introductory notes in the Student Book for Reading, SLC and Writing so that your students are negotiating one aspect of the qualification and their self-assessment at a time. As part of your introduction to the skills checklists, you might encourage them to discuss each aspect (with peers and then as a class) so that they fully understand them. The rating out of 10 and the 'comments' section may also be useful as part of any formative assessment system and individual target setting.

| I can: | I need more work on this 1–4 | I am ok but need a little more work 5–7 | I am confident that I can do this 8–10 | /10 | Comments |
|---|---|---|---|---|---|
| Select and use different types of text | | | | | |
| Obtain information from texts | | | | | |
| Utilise relevant information from texts | | | | | |
| Read and summarise information/ideas from a text | | | | | |
| Read and summarise information/ ideas from different sources | | | | | |
| Identify purposes of texts | | | | | |
| Comment on how meaning is conveyed | | | | | |
| Detect point of view | | | | | |
| Detect implicit meaning | | | | | |
| Detect bias | | | | | |
| Analyse texts in relation to audience needs | | | | | |
| Consider suitable responses | | | | | |

# Skills checklist – Speaking, listening and communication

| I can: | I need more work on this 1–4 | I am ok but need a little more work 5–7 | I am confident that I can do this 8–10 | /10 | Comments |
|---|---|---|---|---|---|
| Consider complex information | | | | | |
| Give a relevant response | | | | | |
| Use appropriate language | | | | | |
| Present information clearly | | | | | |
| Present information persuasively | | | | | |
| Adapt contributions to suit audience | | | | | |
| Adapt contributions to suit purpose | | | | | |
| Adapt contributions to suit situation | | | | | |
| Make significant contributions to discussions | | | | | |
| Take a range of roles | | | | | |
| Help move the discussion forward | | | | | |

# Skills checklist – Writing

| I can: | I need more work on this 1–4 | I am ok but need a little more work 5–7 | I am confident that I can do this 8–10 | /10 | Comments |
|---|---|---|---|---|---|
| Present information/ ideas concisely | | | | | |
| Present information/ ideas logically | | | | | |
| Present information/ ideas persuasively | | | | | |
| Present information on complex subjects clearly | | | | | |
| Present information on complex subjects concisely | | | | | |
| Use different writing styles for different purposes | | | | | |
| Use range of sentences, including complex sentences | | | | | |
| Use paragraphs to organise writing | | | | | |
| Punctuate using commas, apostrophes and inverted commas | | | | | |
| Make sure written work is fit for purpose | | | | | |
| Make sure written work is fit for purpose | | | | | |
| Use accurate spelling and punctuation | | | | | |

# Functional Skills English L2 student book at a glance

## READING

| Skill Standard | | Coverage and range | Student book pages |
|---|---|---|---|
| 1 | Reading different kinds of texts | Learning to choose and use varied types of text for information. | 8–11 |
| 2 | Skimming, scanning and close reading | Reading to suit different purposes: skimming, scanning and close reading of texts. | 12–13 |
| 3 | Finding main ideas and details | Read and summarise succinctly and identify the purposes of texts. | 14–15 |
| 4 | Comparing texts | Read and summarise succinctly, information/ideas from different sources. | 16–17 |
| 5 | Selecting relevant information from more than one text | Select and use different types of texts, and summarise succinctly information/ideas from different sources. | 18–19 |
| 6 | Understanding tables | The use of tables and finding information in them. | 20–21 |
| 7 | Summarising information and ideas | Read and summarise succinctly information/ideas from different sources. | 22–23 |
| 8 | Understanding the purpose of a text | Identify the purposes of texts (and comment on how meaning is conveyed). | 24–25 |
| 9 | How writers communicate meaning | Understanding how writers communicate meaning and recognising the meaning. | 26–27 |
| 10 | Understanding implied meanings | Detect point of view, implicit meaning and/or bias. | 28–29 |
| 11 | Identifying points of view and bias | Detect points of view and bias. | 30–31 |
| 12 | Consider suitable responses to texts | Analyse texts in relation to audience needs and consider suitable responses. | 32–33 |

## SPEAKING, LISTENING AND COMMUNICATION

| Skill Standard | | Coverage and range | Student book pages |
|---|---|---|---|
| 1 | Taking part in discussions | Make significant contributions to discussions, taking a range of roles, and move discussion forward. | 48–51 |
| 2 | Making effective presentations | Planning and preparing a presentation and interaction with the audience. | 52–55 |

# Functional Skills English L2 student book at a glance

## WRITING

| Skill Standard | Coverage and range | Student book pages |
|---|---|---|
| 1 Thinking about your audience | Ensure written work is fit for purpose and audience. | 64–65 |
| 2 Writing to suit a purpose | Understanding writing form and fitting it for purpose. | 66–67 |
| 3 Understanding form | Recognising different styles of writing, for different purposes, and with a reference to being fit for purpose. | 68–73 |
| 4 Understanding style | Understanding various styles of writing and learning to suit own writing for purpose. | 74–75 |
| 5 Writing formal letters | Writing formal letters using form, style and paragraphs effectively. | 76–81 |
| 6 Planning and organising your writing | Learning to effectively plan and organise ideas, presenting complex information clearly. | 82–85 |
| 7 Writing a briefing paper | Researching and understanding a basic structure, and purpose, of a briefing paper. Using apostrophes correctly. | 86–89 |
| 8 Making a convincing argument | Effectively building clear arguments and backing up ideas/opinions with evidence. | 90–93 |
| 9 Writing a report | Writing clear reports, concise in meaning and accurate, with correct spelling and grammar. | 94–99 |

# Approaches to teaching

## Introduction

The Reading section of the Edexcel Functional Skills English Level 2 student book targets all of the skills standards and coverage and range required for the teaching of Level 2 Reading. Reading is divided into 12 sections and each has an introduction, important information presented as *Top tips* and activities designed to develop the skills as described in the Ofqual Functional Skills Subject Criteria.

Each section in the student book forms the basis for the lesson and the purpose is made very clear in the box called *This lesson will help you to*. The tone of each section is directed at students to enable them to engage with the reading activities. Reiterate that the text book will also be a useful revision tool and a reference book in their preparations for the examination.

## The lessons

Page 6 of the student book introduces the Reading section. It details how learners will be assessed, and the 'standards' are also printed for the students so they know what they need to be able to do in order to be considered functional at Level 2.

It is always a good starting point to ask the students to identify the main purpose of a text. This is a feature of our Reading assessment, as exemplified in the sample assessment materials. There are opportunities to make connections between lessons – wherever possible, encourage students to make these links in order to contextualise their reading.

As you take students through the different sections of this book, encourage them to decide which reading skill(s) they need to use to navigate their way around particular texts and how to answer a particular question.

## Helping students to engage with the texts

It is important to teach students how to read texts actively. Encourage them to read with a pencil and annotate (where appropriate) or make brief notes while they are reading. As they become more confident, they can focus on:

- words or phrases that might help them to answer the assessment question
- words they do not know which may need thought when answering the question
- topic sentences that define the subject of a paragraph and help to identify the main points

- connectives that link ideas together, helping them to see the relationship between ideas in a text.

These activities will help them to recognise different features of texts and to shape their own writing according to form, audience and purpose.

## Modelling reading skills

Model reading skills by using an overhead or digital projector.

- Choose a task or question and talk about your thought processes as you read it.
- Explain what reading skills you are using and why.
- Explain how you make sense of difficult words, or words you do not know.
- Show that you sometimes have problems answering questions, but that you can engage with the text in order to work things out.

As you take students through the course, encourage them to co-present with one of their peers and model their own reading skills and thought processes.

## Understanding how texts are organised

With knowledge of the conventional language and presentational features of different text types, students can explore a range of texts and their purposes. Writers will use language and presentational features deliberately for effect, and they collectively influence the message of the text. Encourage learners to ask questions such as:

- What effect does the layout have?
- Why is part of the text presented in columns?
- Why are there sub-headings?
- Do the bullet points help to structure the information to make it easier to find and use?

Encourage students to use strategies for reading tables, using keys, and understanding titles, headings and symbols. Impress upon them that they will need to be able to recognise features of a text in order to consider its purpose, and be able to select and use different types of text as defined in the coverage and range.

## How meaning is conveyed

Encourage learners to focus on the purpose of a text, and how the writer has conveyed meaning to achieve that purpose. Demonstrate how to read 'between the lines' for implied meanings, and interrogate texts for bias and point of view.

## Suitable responses

Writers may want readers to respond in a particular way to their texts. Encourage students to consider the writer's purpose in a text and what the audience's needs may be, before considering suitable responses – the best response may or may not be what the writer intended. Emphasise to students that suitable responses to texts in Functional English is linked with real-life application of reading skills. Invite them to think of examples of this type of text, such as advice/guidance leaflets. It would be useful to provide some practical examples such as guidance on how to complete a passport application. Although the newly accredited qualification differs slightly from the pilot materials, there are past papers which will provide resources to use for this aspect of their reading.

## Preparing for the test

Teach students to read the questions before they start to read the source texts. Looking out for key words in the question will help them to find specific information in the texts. This will mean their reading has a purpose. It is important, however, that learners read the text closely before they begin answering the questions. Use past pilot texts to encourage students to read both texts and questions wisely. Invite them to respond to specific questions and identify which part of the standard is being assessed. Share the mark schemes with them.

Use the mini test provided in the student book and the sample assessment materials as the definitive guidance for your students. Give them practice or 'mock' examination opportunities using these materials so that they become used to managing time and responding appropriately to the questions and the text. Use these practice assessments, sample answers and examiner commentaries in this teacher guide to analyse what the examiners are looking for in terms of functional reading at Level 2.

These materials will also help you and your students to identify areas in which they feel confident and areas where they need more practice in order to refine their reading skills. After they have answered the questions, take them through the mark schemes and any examiner commentaries. Encourage them in pairs/small groups to discuss the answers as indicated in the mark scheme, link the questions with the skills standard and read closely any examiner comments. They might want to highlight key words/concepts to discuss and then to share with others in the group. These types of activities will help them build up confidence, prepare them for the examination and help them to become functional readers in real-life situations.

# 1 Reading different kinds of texts

## Aim
- Learning to choose and use varied types of text for information.

## Lesson learning objectives
- Choose and use different texts to find relevant information.

## Lesson starter
Ask students to think of as many different kinds of texts as they can in 5 minutes and display them on a spider diagram. What makes each text different? Direct students to the start of page 8 in the student book and ensure they focus on purpose as well as function.

## Main teaching and learning
Ask students to look at Text A on page 8 of the student book and answer Activity 1 on the same page. Select students to feed back their answers to the class.

Then, they move on to Activity 2 (on page 9), completing Tasks 1–3 by referring back to the list of features at the beginning of the chapter (page 8) to help them. Ask students to link the features to a specific purpose (e.g. how the top five theme parks are presented in the text).

Give feedback to the class again and continue with Task 4 in Activity 2, if there is time.

## Plenary
Discuss the activities as a class, linking back to the purpose of the lesson and the list of features. Ask students to add any other features that they have specifically identified in terms of making reading different kind of texts accessible.

## Homework
Either complete Task 4 or direct students to find one text by themselves and carry out the same analysis as in the activities above (including: text type, clues, locating information on a page, instructions to the reader, how the first section/paragraph introduces the rest of the text).

# Answers

### Activity 1
This gives the student a pointer on how to start identifying specifics from a text, e.g. here Text A is a letter and the clue is it starts with the greeting 'Sir'.

### Activity 2
1 The first paragraph introduces the troubles the writer has had with chopping onions, which make his sensitive eyes run.

2 a This information is given at the start of the main text: Alton Towers, Thorpe Park, Chessington World of Adventures, Drayton Manor and Legoland Windsor.

  b A sub-heading highlights information about Adventure Island in Southend-on-Sea. It is a free admission park, where you just pay for the rides you go on. The park features roller coasters, such as Green Scream and other rides for the family.

  c The top banner of the website has a search feature with individual 'buttons' for various theme parks where (presumably) more detailed information can be found. Also separate sections for theme parks in England, Scotland and Wales.

3 a The tariff table's third column provides Average Line Rental costs.

  b The tariff table's second column shows and lists the Mobile Phone Model(s), (e.g. here a Nokia 1661).

  c By clicking on the underlined 'Click here for more information on this deal' in the Contract Deal Information column.

4 a The labels identify all the important features that one should have on their door to improve safety.

  b The text in bold gives important information that the reader should consider.

  c The words in CAPITALS label the door safety features.

# 2 Skimming, scanning and close reading

### Aim
- Reading to suit different purposes: skimming, scanning and close reading of texts.

### Lesson learning objectives
- Use different reading skills to find relevant information.

## Lesson starter

Put the three terms (skimming, scanning and close reading) on the board/screen. Students work in pairs or small groups to discuss what they think each term means. Then, direct students to page 12 of the student book to read the explanations. Reinforce the 'functionality' of the skills.

## Main teaching and learning

Students complete Tasks 1–3 in Activity 1, on page 12 of the student book. Afterwards, take class feedback and discuss why these are important skills to learn.

As a class, look at Task 4 combining the two skills scan and close read. The task could be completed in small groups, giving students a few minutes to do this before discussing as a whole class. Ask students why they were given a time limit – relate it to a range of situations where they'll need to read quickly for a specific purpose.

## Plenary

In small groups, students discuss why we need these three main skills in reading and link this with real-life situations.

## Homework

Ask students to find an appropriate text of their own and carry out the above activities, writing their responses and submitting these with their chosen text.

# Answers

### Activity 1

1  Answer C: It explains what the law says every human being's rights are.

2  Freedom to move, freedom of thought and freedom of expression.

3  Answer C: The law is the same for everyone and we all have to be treated fairly.

4  No, people cannot be forced to join a religion or political party.

# ❸ Finding main ideas and details

## Aim
• Read and summarise succinctly and identify the purposes of texts.

## Lesson learning objectives
• Find and use main ideas and details in texts.

## Lesson starter

Introduce the purpose of the lesson and link it with the standards. Make clear the distinction between main ideas and details, as students often find this problematic.

Ask students to look at Text A from page 30 of the student book. They should read the text and note the main idea as well as the details, then discuss the text with a partner, including the differences between the main idea and the details.

Select some students to share ideas about their examples with the class. Reinforce the distinction between main ideas and details.

## Main teaching and learning

Read Text A in Activity 1 on page 14 of the student book. As a class, discuss the four possible statements, listed in Task 2, and decide which one captures the main point of the text and which ones are about the details within the text. Use opportunity to draw their attention to the multiple choice style of the Activity.

Direct students to Text B in Activity 2 on page 15 of the student book and read the text with them. Then, on their own, students write answers to Task 2. Ask them to share their answers with a partner.

Students should then look at Task 3 in small groups and identify the three offers made to teenagers to get them to take part. They should also make brief notes and then discuss the main idea of the text.

## Plenary

Each group shares their responses with the class. Remind students once more of the difference between main ideas and details within a text.

## Homework

Students turn their notes from Activity 2 into properly written answers.

## Answers

### Activity 1
2 Answer B: Panelbase pays people money or gift vouchers for taking surveys.

3 A, C and D are details, rather than the main focus.

### Activity 2
2 Market research companies need teenage opinions to help influence what new products and services are introduced in the future.

3 Three of the things explained can include: cash, High Street vouchers, free CDs, cinema tickets, online music downloads, the chance to win thousands of prizes.

4 That online surveys are the perfect teen job, because they are a safe, free and fun way to earn extra money.

# 4 Comparing texts

## Aim

• Read and summarise succinctly, information/ideas from different sources.

## Lesson learning objectives

• Compare texts. Choose and use different texts to find relevant information.

## Lesson starter

Ask students to discuss what they understand by the instruction to 'compare two different texts'. Take them through the four steps on page 16 of the student book.

Discuss ways that students can make these steps and record their findings (e.g. as spider diagrams). Make it clear that the four steps will be a useful revision aid.

## Main teaching and learning

Direct students to Text A on page 17 of the student book and read it with them. Ask them to list or highlight the main idea and the details. Do the same with Text B on the same page.

Students go through the tasks in Activity 1, on page 16. In feedback, focus on the words 'similar' and 'different' to encourage students to compare and contrast. Students should list differences and similarities.

## Plenary

Return to the Task 3 in Activity 1. Ask students to share with another pair their views regarding how Texts A and B are presented. Ask for feedback from the class. It might be necessary to use the plenary to draw students' attention to text features, contexts and purposes, as well as language and information, in preparation for the homework.

## Homework

Students to present their findings on both texts in three parts.

1 Similarities in terms of subject and structure of texts.

2 Differences in terms of subject and structure of texts.

3 Differences and similarities in how texts are presented.

## Answers

### Activity 1

1 Answer A: There is only one way to score a goal in football.

2 A, B and C

3 a Both games have certain rules for scoring.
   b Each game has different ways of scoring points.

# 5 Selecting relevant information from more than one text

## Aim
- Select and use different types of texts, and summarise succinctly information/ideas from different sources.

## Lesson learning objectives
- Choose and use different texts to find relevant information.

## Lesson starter

As in previous lessons, direct students to the four steps to selecting relevant information (on page 18 of the student book) and read it with them.

## Main teaching and learning

Students read Texts A, B, C, on page 19, and decide the text types for each one.

They then complete Task 1 (a, b and c) in Activity 1 on page 18. Remind students to think about previous lessons, where they identified the main ideas and their details. Ensure they look at the organisational features of the texts, including layout and language. Feed back as a class.

Students read the profiles of Ash and Emily (page 18) and list the main ideas in each profile, in bullet points. Revisiting Texts A, B and C, they should link information from the profiles with information about the Fifteen Foundation and decide who should be selected to become an apprentice and why.

Draw their attention to how we make judgements in real life and how, to some extent, their decision in this activity was a matter of opinion.

## Plenary

Discuss the decisions made, e.g. What key pieces of information led to their decision? Which texts did students use to select relevant information? Was any one text particularly useful?

## Homework

Students select relevant information from another text (either one from earlier in the student book or one of their choice).

## Answers

### Activity 1
1 a  Text B
   b  Text C
   c  Text A

2 b  Emily is more qualified to become an apprentice because she 'loves cooking'.

# ⑥ Understanding tables

## Aim
• The use of tables and finding information in them.

## Lesson learning objectives
• Use tables to find relevant information.

## Lesson starter

Students think of all the different text types that they have encountered in the past week and list them on a spider diagram. Discuss the different texts as a class and lead students to consider how they use tables. What types of table do they see and use outside of the learning context?

Remind students of the four steps as guidance from the previous lesson. Direct them to page 20 of the student book and take them through the four instructions supplied to help them to 'read' a table.

## Main teaching and learning

Take students through the description of Josh's requirements at the beginning of Activity 1 (page 20). Connect his situation of being in an unfamiliar place to real-life contexts.

Ask students to list his requirements and list the type of information Josh needs to be able to book his hotel.

Students work through Tasks 1–4. Then, students feed back their answers and discuss as a class. Finally, do the same for Tasks 5–7.

## Plenary

Emphasise the need to understand texts in their broadest sense (e.g. tables) and relate this to being functional in real life. Why do we need to be able to read and understand tables?

## Homework

Ask students to look at another example of a table (provide this for them, if possible) and highlight key areas of information to be found in it.

## Answers

### Activity 1
1 All of them except the Campanile Hotel Manchester, which is 0.8 miles away.

2 The Midlands Qhotels, Velvet Hotel, The Palace Hotel, Radisson Edwardian Manchester, Abode Manchester, The Lowry A Rocco Forte Hotel.

3 The Palace Hotel

4 Answer C: Velvet Hotel

5 0.1 and 0.4 miles.

6 Answer B: (In the table, on 8 January, the least expensive hotel is Days Hotel Manchester City, at £35.00/night, which is 0.6 miles from the city centre.)

7 The Midland Qhotels or The Palace Hotel.

Student book pages 22–23

# 7 Summarising information and ideas

## Aim
• Read and summarise succinctly information/ideas from different sources.

## Lesson learning objectives
• Read and briefly summarise information and ideas from different texts.

## Lesson starter

Provide each student with a copy of the coverage and range, listed above. Ask students to identify what is being required of them by underlining/circling key words. Discuss until you have covered the following:

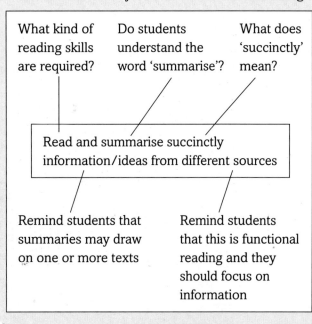

What kind of reading skills are required?

Do students understand the word 'summarise'?

What does 'succinctly' mean?

Read and summarise succinctly information/ideas from different sources

Remind students that summaries may draw on one or more texts

Remind students that this is functional reading and they should focus on information

## Main teaching and learning

Direct students to read the text on summarising at the start of page 22 of the student book, then ask them to work through Activity 1. Remind them to use the advice in point 3 of the teaching text to help them, and the notes in the *Watch Out!* box to avoid common mistakes. For less able students, ask for a list of key facts under the questions given in the student book, and then scaffold write the summary in up to 50 words, referring to the *Watch Out!* tip. Repeat the process for further texts, either by working through Activity 2 or by using your own text choices.

Ask students to feed back to others in a group to establish the following.

• The main ideas/information in each text.
• How to present the ideas/information identified in each of the texts in short focused statements, using the questions given.

## Plenary

Students share their responses with the class. Why is it important to be able to respond to texts in this way in order to be functional in today's society? Ask students to consider when this might be necessary, for example, in the workplace. Then, discuss and reinforce what is being asked of the student when assessed on this skills standard.

## Self/peer assessment

Direct students back to the coverage and range and the learning objectives on page 22. How confident are they of their skills in reading and summarising one or more texts? What needs more practice?

## Answers

**Activity 1**
Students use the question words to pick out information, then write a short summary of Text A.

**Activity 2**
Possible answers could include: gives young people 'a chance' for 'good futures'.

Student book pages 24–25

# ⑧ Understanding the purpose of a text

### Aim
- Identify the purposes of texts (and comment on how meaning is conveyed).

### Lesson learning objectives
- Work out and understand the purpose of a text.

## Lesson starter

Draw students' attention to the coverage and range for this lesson. They discuss their understanding of the term 'purpose'. Explain how we make judgements about a writer's purpose and the importance of supporting these judgements with evidence from the text.

Direct students to page 24 of the student book. Look at the three steps to use when reading to establish the purpose of a text. Take them through each of the steps, explaining what they entail, prior to moving on to the main part of the lesson.

## Main teaching and learning

Students read Text A and use the steps 1, 2, and 3 to establish the purpose. Point out the layout of the text and how it links with its purpose, e.g. is it to advise and inform about 'sunshine safe skin' or is there any suggestion of persuasive language? Remind students that they must provide evidence from the text to support their ideas.

Students then decide which statement best describes the purpose of Text B. Are there any other thoughts/ideas?

Direct students back to the texts on pages 9–11 of the student book (theme parks, safety leaflet extract and mobile phone tariff) and then they complete Activity 2.

## Plenary

Feed back to the class and agree the purpose of each of the texts on pages 9–11. What strategies did students use to establish the purpose of each text?

## Answers

### Activity 1
1  A possible answer might be:
   This text looks like a magazine article, written to give advice to people who want to spend time in the sun.

2  Text B is an advert for inflatable wigs, despite having been written in an overtly 'chummy' way.

### Activity 2
1  Text B on page 9 is a guide to the UK theme parks. Text C on page 10 is a pricelist/tariff list for mobile phones. Text D on page 11 is a safety leaflet.

# ⑨ How writers communicate meaning

## Aim

- Understanding how writers communicate meaning and recognising the meaning.

## Lesson learning objectives

- Comment on how a writer communicates the meaning of a text.

## Lesson starter

Link this lesson with previous work on identifying the purpose of a text. Take students through the three steps on page 26 of the student book to prepare them for the lesson. Then direct them back to Text A, on page 25. They should then revisit this article and apply the three steps. Get feedback as a whole class.

Ask the question: 'Why is it important to appreciate how writers communicate meaning and the features that they use?'

## Main teaching and learning

Students work through Activity 1, completing Tasks 1 and 2. Take feedback from the class. Ensure that they explain the effect of each feature.

Then, they write an individual response to Task 3. Allow approximately 10–15 minutes before some class discussion.

After the discussion, students go through Tasks 4 and 5, making brief notes and discussing. Take feedback from the whole class.

Put students in small groups and direct them to complete Activity 2. Discuss the purpose of each of the texts on page 17 (work from previous lesson may be used as support). Review the texts and suggest any changes that might make meaning and purpose clearer to the reader.

## Plenary

Each group feeds back to the class by recording their ideas on flip chart paper or on an interactive whiteboard.

## Homework

Complete Activity 1 (Tasks 1–5) again, this time based on the texts on page 17. This activity will be useful for revision purposes.

# Answers

### Activity 1

1. Its purpose is to persuade people to take part in the bike rides.

2. a  All features are used except bullet points and lists.
   b  Heading – tells the reader the name of the event and the date.

      Image – interesting image of a mountain biker to grab the reader's attention.

      Caption – adds detail to the image.

      Paragraphs – break the text up and make it easier to read.

      Pull-out box – highlights a key piece of information.

3. The first two paragraphs make the event sound appealing to the reader by talking about the natural beauty of the moors. The third paragraph gives more detail about the length of the rides, and the final one repeats that it is a 'must-do' experience.

4. The writer uses words that would appeal to cyclists, such as 'hills are a carpet of purple heather', 'splendour' and 'toughest'.

5. *Any answers are based on opinions and observations, so model answers are not supplied here.*

### Activity 2

Check that the responses to this group work task are relevant and sensible.

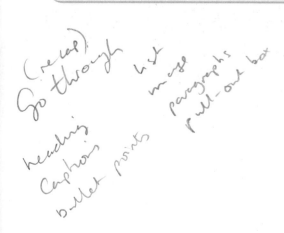

# 10 Understanding implied meanings

## Aim
- Detect point of view, implicit meaning and/or bias.

## Lesson learning objectives
- Understand meanings that are hinted at or suggested. Be able to identify facts and opinions.

## Lesson starter

Students discuss what is meant by the term 'implied meaning' and feed back to the class. How is this different from obvious meaning? Give them the words from the skill standard. Read the opening paragraph on page 28 of the student book together.

Look at the text from the tourism website (in the introduction part on page 28). Ask students the following:

1  What is the text telling you?
2  How are omissions also informative?

Empty out the phrase 'fabulous shopping allied to some magnificent hotels' either through class discussion or initially in pairs. Draw students' attention to the *Watch out!* box on page 28 and take them through the advice given.

## Main teaching and learning

In pairs, students discuss and list ideas that are linked with the myth of Santa Claus. Feed back to the class and list ideas on the board.

Read Text A together. Students complete Activity 1 in groups, using the ideas about Santa Claus with both of the questions where it is helpful. Which of statements A–E is obvious and which are implied?

Students do Activity 2. Ask students to find evidence to support their choice and read the *Watch out!* advice on page 28 of the student book. Ask students to discuss why recognising implied meaning is an important life skill.

## Plenary

Decide the main purpose of the Text A through a class discussion (it is an advertisement using the myth of Santa Claus in a humorous way).

## Homework

Students re-read Texts A and B, and write the implied meanings separately for each, giving evidence from the texts to support their ideas.

# Answers

### Activity 1
1  a  'After centuries of reading the world's begging letters, trespassing on private property, stuffing socks and eating stale mince pies –'
   b  'There was a time when folks would make do with a satsuma and a pair of newly darned socks.'
   c  'This is the sort of fancy pants gear so-called hipsters go gaga for.'
2  Statement C, because the advert implies that Carphone Warehouse have the best products and that not even Santa can keep up.

### Activity 2
Statement A is an Opinion.
Statement B is a Fact.
Statement C is a Fact. *(Although 'spacious lounge' could be an opinion.)*
Statement D is an Opinion.
Statement E is a Fact.

# 11 Identifying points of view and bias

## Aim
• Detect points of view and bias.

## Lesson learning objectives
• Recognise points of view and bias, understand how these can affect meaning.

## Lesson starter

Take students through the introduction on page 30 of the student book. Link this with previous lessons on identifying main purpose and also with the skill(s) coverage.

Students think of any other words linked with feelings, beliefs and thoughts. Ask them to consider whether the words link with texts containing facts or texts containing opinion. Bring out that a viewpoint is an opinion. Students also need to be aware that sometimes opinions and viewpoints are presented as facts.

## Main teaching and learning

Read Text A together (page 30 in the student book). Students then work to complete Activity 1. They should also consider the purpose of the article – leading up to party action regarding advertisements aimed at under-16s.

Feed back as a class, then read Text B together. Students complete Activity 2 before feeding back to the class again.

Then look at Activity 3. Students decide which of the three texts presents a balanced point of view and which has bias – and what kind. Ensure they use evidence to support their ideas.

*Additional activity*: if in an IT room, students could select a different article that has points of view/bias, to share in the plenary.

## Plenary

Students feed back their thoughts about the three texts to the class. They may feel that bias is evident in all of them.

## Homework

Students find their own short article and complete these two tasks.

1 Select words and phrases that reveal a writer's point of view.
2 Identify the evidence used by the writer to support that viewpoint, which can be presented in the form of a table.

# Answers

### Activity 1
1 a Possible answers include:
'unrealistic', 'unattainable images', 'protect children', 'digitally manipulated shapes and sizes'.

b Answer B: Airbrushed images put pressure on young people who think that is how they should look.

### Activity 2
1 a Words and phrases can include 'Is that really fair?', 'I don't want to be 'skinny'; just fit and healthy', 'Moss is not wrong to say that you feel better if you are slim'.

b Evidence includes 'a quarter of Britons are obese', 'It is the poor…who are fat' and 'our culture has a very sick underbelly'.

### Activity 3
1 a Text B presents a more balanced point of view, while Text A is biased.

b Text A is biased because it aims to persuade rather than inform the reader.

2 The text has been written for teenage magazine readers; the writer assumes the reader shares their opinion.

# 12 Consider suitable responses to texts

## Aim
- Analyse texts in relation to audience needs and consider suitable responses.

## Lesson learning objectives
- Consider texts in terms of the writer's purpose and the readers' needs. Work out what a suitable response to a text is.

## Lesson starter

Share the skill standard with the students, discussing with them how the ability to analyse texts and consider suitable responses are important for real-life situations.

Introduce the lesson by taking students through the introduction on page 32 of the student book.

Direct students to go back to Text B on page 31 and carry out the following:
1 Re-read the text.
2 Go through the six questions on page 32 (in the introduction part) noting their answers.

A brief class discussion before moving on to the main section of the lesson.

## Main teaching and learning

Direct students to read Text A on page 32 and then complete Activity 1. Pause after they have answered a, b and c and briefly discuss their answers as a class. At the end of the activity, ask students which part of the skill standard they think they have covered.

Before starting Activity 2, close the student book. In pairs, students list the features that they would expect to find in a business letter from a consultant for an international company. Return to page 33 of the student book and read Text B together.

Put students back in their pairs to complete the activity. Students decide which statement best sums up the writer's purpose. Take feedback halfway through.

## Plenary

As a class, discuss if the reader should respond to this letter and apply for the job. Discuss reasons for the agreed response. What is a suitable response for the reader to make to this letter? Make sure students understand the term 'fit for purpose'.

## Homework

Students write a suitable response to Text B. Their own responses need to be appropriate and any temptation to respond in kind should be discouraged!

## Answers

### Activity 1
1 a To help people avoid being scammed.
  b Anyone old enough to accept offers or prizes.
  c **and** d Yes, it is detailed and clearly written for its purpose, which is to advise and warn.
  e 'catch you unawares', 'slick and professional', 'rush you'
  f Yes, as it would help them know what to look out for.

### Activity 2
1 a To claim to help the reader make money.
  b Headed paper, contact details, correct spelling and grammar. This letter does not have these.
  c The reader should not respond. The letter is badly written and asks for the reader's name and contact details, without giving any of the company's own.

# Approaches to teaching

## Introduction

There are two distinct areas of assessment in this component. Students are assessed for performance in a discussion and for delivering a presentation. Once students are fully prepared, these assessments must take place at properly designated times, rather than an 'opportunistic' assessment of a student's skills in the context of another learning activity.

You could begin in a similar manner as for Reading. Use the introductory pages of the student book to show your students the skill standard, the coverage and range and the two aspects of the assessment. Emphasise that they need to be proficient in both discussion and presentation. As your students grow in confidence, familiarise them with the assessment grids so that they know the criteria on which their assessment will be based.

## The lessons

In both the Reading and Writing lessons, students are given a range of opportunities to discuss aspects of their learning and feed back their comments to the larger group. You could use these activities to help your students prepare for their speaking, listening and communication assessments. When they are presenting their ideas, encourage them to use different resources so that they are familiar with different approaches before they deliver their presentation for assessment in this component. They could use slides, large annotated texts for display purposes and audio-visual resources where appropriate.

Pages 46 to 55 of the student book have detailed resources to help your students prepare fully for speaking, listening and communication assessments. The lesson plans provided are based upon this student resource but you may wish to divide the activities into smaller sections, depending upon length of lessons and the needs of your learners.

Your students need to be aware that the assessment covers participation in a discussion and delivery of a presentation and that they need to show that they are functional in both aspects. The self-assessment grid breaks down the coverage and range into separate strands so that students can recognise areas of strength and areas for development.

## Participation in discussions

Consider a range of contexts for the discussions and encourage your students to choose their own areas for discussion.

Through their preparations for assessment direct them to ensure that:
- they make contributions to the discussions – this may be as a question for clarification or a comment in response to others
- their responses indicate that they have been listening – they could be encouraged to show this by beginning 'the point you just made about…'
- they take a variety of roles as part of their preparation – for example, have they chaired a discussion? Taken on the role of an interviewer/interviewee?
- Their body language is positive – eye contact, facing those in discussion, avoiding folding arms, gazing into space/out of the window.

Emphasise that these are life skills and how important it is in real-life situations to be able to exhibit speaking, listening and communication skills and related, positive behaviours.

## Delivering a presentation

Use the presentational type activities from the lessons for Reading and Writing as a basis for developing the ability of each learner to deliver a presentation. During the course of the Reading and Writing lessons your learners will deliver feedback to others, present annotated texts and participate in small group and class discussions related to a particular part of their learning.

As stated in our specification, students may deliver a presentation with other learners but their contribution must be significant so that they demonstrate their functionality in all aspects of the coverage and range. They must also ensure that their preparation of the presentation is equal to that of others involved.

Through their preparations for delivering a presentation, direct them to ensure that:
- they are comfortable with the resources that they use to deliver their presentation
- they are not overly-reliant on the resources so that, for example, there are an excessive number of slides and that they simply read them
- they engage with the audience and use any notes as support only
- they do not simply read a script
- their presentation has a persuasive element to it
- they have a clear sense of purpose in their chosen subject for presentation
- they control the timing of their presentation
- they provide opportunities for any questions.

It is a requirement of the skill standard that some of the contexts are unfamiliar. You might want to decide how this will be achieved. For example, does discussion take place with a visitor to your centre? Is the presentation delivered to a different group of people from their usual teaching group?

## Use of a dictionary

You will have noted that dictionaries are allowed in both the Reading and Writing assessments in Functional English. This is because in the real world we acknowledge that there are times when we could and should use a dictionary to check the spelling and/or meaning of a word. Some students make efficient use of it as a resource and others spend most of their time attempting to navigate their way around it, with limited success. In a significant number of cases, students disregard the dictionary as a valuable resource that will help them to be more functional across the three components. Much of this lack of effective use of the dictionary is due to students lacking confidence and experience. The use of the dictionary should be an accepted part of life. Students need to be encouraged to use the dictionary throughout the course so that it becomes part of being functional in language in a real-life context.

Encourage students to use the dictionary in the following situations:
- Looking up the meanings of key words in the Functional Skills Criteria.
- Looking up meanings of words in reading texts and writing stimulus.
- Looking up meanings of words in questions.
- When preparing for writing tasks as presented in the student book, particularly in the sections focussing on technical skills.

You may have to remind students of the layout of a dictionary, even providing a copy of the alphabet in the initial stages of the course to activate prior knowledge and reinforce something with which they should be readily familiar. Again, that this is a valuable life skill is worth reinforcing.

There are many ways to use dictionaries in your lessons. You could add to suggested starter activities by providing words for your learners to look up in their dictionaries – this could have a competitive edge to it and might involve students competing to see who can find the answer first. Alternatively, you could be asking them to look for meaning. These activities could be separate from the main body of the lesson, but it is usually educationally sound to link any dictionary work with the lesson itself as learning is more effective when contextualised.

Student book pages 48–51

# 1 Taking part in discussions

## Aim

- Make significant contributions to discussions, taking a range of roles and move discussion forward.

## Lesson learning objectives

- Plan and prepare a group discussion. Take a range of roles in formal group discussion.

## Lesson starter

Share the skills standards with the students, then provide them with statements for group discussion. With a partner, they discuss which of these they agree/disagree with and share ideas in class feedback.

- Make sure that your point of view is always heard
- Make cogent responses and use appropriate tone according to the context.
- Make sure that you spend most of the time listening.

Ask students in pairs to decide what they think are the differences between formal and informal discussion.

## Plenary

Students share findings about group performance with the class and discuss what they think needs to be improved. There are likely to be some areas that are common across the groups and some differences that can be shared in the plenary.

## Homework

Students should find another topic for discussion, then for homework set out their chosen subject in a Situation box similar to the one on page 48.

## Main teaching and learning

Take students through Steps 1 and 2 on student book page 48. Direct students to read the details given in the box entitled *Situation*. Then with a partner, pull out the key points of this situation, which are:

- parenting lessons for 14-year-olds
- content of the lessons
- views about this as a course of action.

Brief feed back to the class before moving on to Activity 2.

Direct students to read the information in Texts A to G on page 49 and discuss whether or not they and their partner agree in this. After that, the pairs group together with another pair and share their ideas.

Take students through Step 3 on page 48 and the *Top tip*, linking this with the standards.

Direct students to go back into pairs and use two points from the previous activity and see how they can use some of these phrases on page 50 to introduce their own ideas.

Students then share some examples with the whole class. Move on to Activity 3 on page 51. They discuss 1a and 1b and make a note of the ideas raised.

Students should review their discussion and feed back to the class a review of the discussion so far.

They should continue formal discussion and as a group reach a final decision about parenting classes for 14-year-olds.

# 2 Making effective presentations

## Aim

- Planning and preparing a presentation and interaction with the audience.

## Lesson learning objectives

- Plan, prepare and give a well-organised presentation, tailored to your audience. Listen carefully and respond to questions from your audience.

## Lesson starter

First, share the skills standard with the students, drawing out the importance of presentations in real-life contexts. Then, ask students to form pairs and think about a few main points on: What makes an effective presentation? Feed back as class.

Ask students to read the *Situation* box on student book page 52. Then, direct students to go through Step 1 and make decisions on feeding back to class the following information: What is the presentation about? Who is the audience? What do they already know? What is the purpose of the presentation?

## Plenary

Students think about ten top tips for delivering an effective presentation, for future reference, and share with the class.

## Homework

Ask students to rehearse their presentations, asking them to consider Steps 6 and 7: advice about giving the presentation and being a listener/member of the audience.

## Main teaching and learning

Discuss how to make the presentation more interesting and add to the ideas suggested in Step 2. Feed back to the class.

After this, go onto Activity 2 on page 52, asking students to work individually and plan a presentation using the table within the activity as a starting point. Encourage the students to use the table 'checklist', as well as the ideas shared with the partner and class earlier, to help with their own ideas.

Individually go through Activity 3 on student book page 53. Set out ideas in a flowchart, adding notes to go with the materials. Direct students to look at words and phrases in the box provided and discuss/practise these with a partner.

Finalise a first draft of the presentation looking at key messages and supporting points.

With a partner, think about and discuss how to use visual aids to support the presentation. Direct students to look at the *Remember* box at the bottom of page 53 and discuss the possible disadvantages of using visual aids in presentations.

Take students through Step 4: Using the right language. Students discuss what is meant by the term 'standard English'. Provide students with text containing non-standard English forms. Direct them to identify the words/phrases and suggest a standard English replacement.

After the discussion, ask students to practise presentation with a partner, whose role is to stop the presentation when non-standard English is used. Every time this happens, the pairs should collaboratively think of how to improve the language and which phrases to use.

# Approaches to teaching

## Introduction

The Writing section of the student book provides opportunities for learners to practise their writing skills in a variety of functional, real-life contexts. The resources and the activities are designed so that the skills acquired are transferable to different real-life situations where writing is required, as well as providing your students with the tools needed to become functional writers at Level 2.

The introductory page to the writing section of the student book provides your learners with the 'standards' needed at Level 2. You might want to put these on an OHT/white board and ask learners to work in pairs/small groups looking at each of the standards in detail. Discuss what is required of students in order that they might successfully meet the standards.

## The lessons

It is useful to draw the attention of your students to the assessment requirements of Level 2 Writing. As with Reading, direct students around the layout of each section of the student book, including the signposting of lesson purpose and the *Top tip* sections.

There are questions provided in the student book for students to practise their writing skills. The sample assessment materials are also a key resource and it is useful to take students through the mark schemes once they have completed the tasks. Examiner's comments on a selection of pass and fail answers are also a useful teaching tool.

Although the Writing lessons are broken down into smaller, more manageable areas, it is useful to encourage your learners to make links between the lessons. For example, audience and purpose are inextricably linked, as are form and style.

There are many opportunities in the lesson plans for students to explore different aspects of writing, both individually and collaboratively. It is useful also for students to use the reading texts in the Reading section of the student book to inform the development of their own writing skills and to reinforce the different forms of writing and their inherent features.

## Modelling writing skills

It may be useful as part of the process to model different aspects of writing skills using an OHT/digital projector. Some of the initial teaching materials from the KS3

National Literacy Strategy are a useful resource for the teaching of writing skills.

## Planning their writing

Section 6 of the Student Book, *Planning and organising your writing*, is very important. Past experience shows that some students avoid planning and organising their written responses, due in part to considering planning as a low priority. The lesson plans suggest ways that your students may work collaboratively. They can then feed back to the class how they have planned their response, and equally importantly, their reasons for structuring their responses in a particular way. You can also model your own thought processes when you plan how you will write a particular document. Return to the reading texts to reinforce the features of different forms. Another link between the reading and their own writing is the consideration of suitable responses to texts.

## Technical aspects of writing

The technical aspects of writing such as spelling, punctuation and grammar are covered throughout the different units of the student book. In order to help the students embed technical skills in their own writing and spelling, punctuation and grammar are contextualised. Contextualisation of the mechanics of language is regarded as good pedagogical practice because students are more likely to be aware of the need to write accurately and check their work if technical accuracy is seen as an inherent feature of writing a fit for purpose document. While it is important that students sustain their form, style and purpose, the technical aspects of writing comprise at least 40% of any assessment. Encourage your students to keep returning to the standards and refer to them as they prepare and then produce their own writing. Provide opportunities in the lessons for students to present annotated texts to exemplify the coverage and range of functional writing at Level 2.

If possible use examples of writing, including technical aspects, by showing them onscreen using either an OHT or a digital projector, and talking the students through the processes of writing, including style, form and purpose. Another way to reinforce writing skills for Level 2 Functional English is to display annotated texts and writing in the teaching area. This will enable your students to make links across all the Writing and Reading lessons. Enlarged copies of the standards with explanatory annotations are also useful teaching tools.

# 🗋 Thinking about your audience

## Aim
- Ensure written work is fit for purpose and audience.

## Lesson learning objectives
- Suit the content and style of your writing to your audience.

## Lesson starter

As a class, read through the introduction on page 64 of the student book. Direct students to read the instruction on writing a letter to a chairperson and how the sense of audience is decided.

Students now look at this task:

> Your local member of parliament has asked for views about raising the school leaving age to eighteen.
>
> Write a letter to your MP giving your views on this idea.
>
> Students should use the steps as suggested on page 64 and decide the following:
> 1 Who is the audience?
> 2 What do they need to know?
> 3 What content and style are needed?

Remind them to use the advice from the *Top tip* box (on page 64) and include a note about audience when they are planning their writing. Whole class discussion follows.

## Main teaching and learning

Students work through Activity 1. In pairs they look at Task 1, statements a and b and decide:
1 The possible audience.
2 What the task tells you about the audience. Make an educated guess about what the audience is like and what they need.
3 Complete the table for tasks A and B (see Task 2).

Discuss as a whole class, repeating for statements c and d.

Students then complete Tasks 3–5 in pairs.

## Plenary

Students share their ideas about Task 5 with the class. What sort of amendments needed to be made to change the jottings into a final draft? Emphasise what we mean by sense of audience.

## Homework

Students take their draft paragraph home and write this up in its final format, still paying attention to audience. Stress that quality is more important than quantity at this stage.

# Answers

### Activity 1
1 a  Your friend who wants to borrow money.
  b  Parents thinking about their children's diets.
  c  The catering manager of the canteen.
  d  People in your area, who buy the newspaper.

**Activities 2–5** *are open student writing tasks, for which answers here have not been supplied.*

Student book pages 66–67

# 2 Writing to suit a purpose

**Aim**
- Understanding writing form and fitting it for purpose.

**Lesson learning objectives**
- Suit your content and style to the purpose of your writing.

## Lesson starter

Ask students to think about reasons why we write in the real world – what different purposes are there for writing? Feed back as a class.

Link real-life writing with functional writing and the importance of being able to construct a written response as a life skill. Take students through the introduction on page 66 of the student book.

## Main teaching and learning

Students read Tasks a, b and c and identify the purpose of each one. They could use flip chart paper and present their ideas to the class.

They should do the same for Tasks d and e, then present responses to the class. Now that the purpose for each task is established, they should decide the features required and add this to the purpose as a spider diagram.

Students read Tunmise's plan on page 67 in preparation for Task e. They decide what she should write in her email and how she should write it. Then they go back to Task a and, using Tunmise's 'notes' as a model, they write their own plan.

Reinforce the message that plans are very useful when writing answers. Once students have finished, they share their ideas with a group and discuss the importance of planning a written response.

## Plenary

Feed back groups' plans for Task A to the whole class.

## Homework

Students choose one other task from Activity 1 and write this out as an individual assignment. Ensure they remember the purpose for the task and as much as possible, sustain this throughout the response.

## Answers

**Activity 1**
1  a  To introduce a new sport of your choice into the curriculum.
   b  To add to a discussion about the legal driving age.
   c  To persuade the council to offer more facilities.
   d  To put forward your view of social networking sites.
   e  To give a holiday company advice about appealing to families.

2  Features should be relevant to the purpose of each task.

3  and 4 are both open student writing activities, but students need to ensure relevant feaures ae included.

# ❸ Understanding form

## Aim
- Recognising different styles of writing, for different purposes, and with a reference to being fit for purpose.

## Lesson learning objectives
- Choose the right form for your writing, and include the features of different forms in your writing.

## Lesson starter

Students discuss with a partner what is meant by the term 'form'. Feed back as a class.

Go through introduction on page 68 of the student book and link this lesson to the relevant section of the skill standard. Direct students to the *Top tip* and explain that the revision cards will be useful to help them understand the different forms of writing.

## Main teaching and learning

There is a lot to cover in this lesson so give firm timings for each part of the activity. Feed back after students have looked at each text, but restrict feedback to a few contributions per section to ensure that the lesson moves on.

### Activity 1

Students read Text A, the report. What are the features of this form? They copy out and complete the labels. Feed back as a class. Work through Texts B–E, varying your approach to how students access each one. Collective filling-in a whiteboard or flip chart as a class or in small groups would work well.

Direct students to make their own revision cards, including checklists and diagrams of features. They then work in pairs to compare their revision cards for each form and test each other. After this, ask pairs to form small groups with others and then carry out the same activity. Encourage them to modify their own ideas about forms and features according to what they learn from each other. Finally, feed back as a class.

### Activity 2

Students match the tasks with the form that they think is most suitable, then record their ideas on a flip chart as preparation for the plenary.

As an individual assignment, each student chooses one of the tasks and writes a brief plan. They should remember to show the features of the form that they would need to include in their response. Swap with a partner and discuss the form and features.

Join up with another partner and share each of the plans, the chosen forms and the features of those forms.

## Plenary

Students share their ideas with the class. Summarise key findings with the class.

## Homework

Using their plan, students write the first two paragraphs of their chosen task. They label the features that they have included in their chosen form.

# Answers

*There are no specific, 'correct' answers for this section. The student book pages 69–73 presents various forms of text and their features, as listed here:*

Text A: is a **Report**

Text B: is a **Briefing paper**

Text C: is a **Magazine article**

Text D: is **Persuasive text**

Text E: is a **Formal letter**

Student book pages 74–75

# 4 Understanding style

### Aim

• Understanding various styles of writing and learning to suit own writing for purpose.

### Lesson learning objectives

• Write in a style that is suited to your purpose and audience.

## Lesson starter

Share the learning objective with the class and ask students to decide what they think is meant by style. How might this link with the previous writing lesson on purpose? Discuss as a class.

Ask students to look at the tasks and the styles in the examples table on page 74 of the student book.

Direct them to look at the different responses and identify:
1 the differences between the responses
2 the possible reasons for the differences.

Discuss as a class and ensure students link style with audience and purpose. Bring out the need to adapt style according to purpose and audience.

Then students decide on style and draft examples for the following:
1 a letter for a job application
2 an email to a friend about the plans for the weekend.

## Main teaching and learning

For the first task of Activity 1, suggest that students set out their responses in a table, for texts A, B, C, D from Task 2 (on page 75), complete with purpose, audience and style recorded. This will help them to order their ideas and understand how the three considerations interrelate. (Please note that since the student book went to press, the Department for Children, Schools and Families has been replaced by the Department for Education.)

Students complete Tasks 1 and 2 in pairs, then individually do Tasks 3 and 4, using Sam's notes to write a first draft for Task A in an appropriate style for the intended purpose. They then swap with a partner and discuss what changes were made and why, before completing Task 5.

## Plenary

Feed back as a class. Discuss the challenges of writing in a particular style and how changes were made to improve the writing drafts.

## Homework

Students choose either B or D in Task 2, and write the first draft of an opening paragraph using what has been learned in this lesson. Direct them back to their table from earlier, as it will help them with this task.

# Answers

### Activity 1

1 and 2
a To inform the DCSF about your view on advertising. Formal, standard English.

b To give information to young people who are considering taking a gap year. Less formal, standard English.

c To give parents information about young people's eating habits. Formal, standard English.

d To give your friend some advice. Less formal, standard English.

**Activities 3–5** are open student writing tasks, for which answers here have not been supplied.

# 5 Writing formal letters

## Aim
- Writing formal letters using form, style and paragraphs effectively.

## Lesson learning objectives
- Write a well organised formal letter and email, use paragraphs effectively, and ensure meaning is clear by using connectives effectively.

## Lesson starter

Take students through the guidance on page 76 of the student book. Direct them to the *Top tip* on the same page and ask them to pay particular attention to formal letter conventions as well as email communications. Throughout the lesson, students should be encouraged to discuss the functionality of their tasks and how what they are learning is relevant in a real-life context, as well as valuable examination preparation.

Students look closely at the letter to the MP on page 77 of the student book. They identify features of a formal letter and if there are any aspects of the letter that could be improved.

On flip chart paper, draw a diagram of how a formal letter should be presented. Emphasise the importance of using paragraphs in their written responses.

Students then carry out the same activity for the email on page 80. Feed back as a class and discuss the differences between a formal letter and an email.

## Main teaching and learning

*(This is a fairly large unit on letter writing, so the potential division points of the lesson into two parts have been identified below.)*

In pairs/small groups, students complete the rest of Activity 1 on page 76. They make a flowchart to show main points and sequencing. Then, in pairs, discuss the effectiveness of the introduction and conclusion. Are there any aspects of the letter that could be improved?

Look at how the writer makes the letter appealing and find the persuasive features used. This is an important part of students' understanding. With a partner, they link the features listed in Task 3b with the letter itself and find examples of each. Feed back and share as a class.

*(Possible end of lesson.)*

*(Possible part two of the lesson.)*

Individually, students complete Tasks 1–4 of Activity 2 (page 78 of the student book). Then with a partner, they swap drafts and read for form, features used and persuasive techniques.

Take students through the structuring of ideas guidance in the PEEL section on page 79. Then in pairs, they look back to the formal letter on page 77 and complete Activities 1 and 2 on page 79. Discuss the areas identified in Task 1c where writers sometimes alter the structure and whether this makes the writing more or less effective. Feedback as a class. Look again at another student's draft to look at how PEEL is used. Note any possible changes that could be made to own work.

Move on to page 80 of the student book and read through the introduction to clear meaning – connectives, including the *Top tip* on the same page.

Students complete Task 1 of Activity 1 on page 80, individually, grouping connectives in a table like the one shown. They then work in small groups/pairs and complete Tasks 2–5.

## Plenary

Discuss how to use PEEL, the uses of different connectives in the email exercise and the purpose of these activities in relation to writing a formal letter. Revisit key points about writing a formal letter and discuss the importance of writing according to audience and purpose and relate to real-life contexts.

## Homework

Using what has been learned throughout the lesson, students complete a final version of their letter.

## Answers

**Activity 1** *is an open student writing task, for which answers have not been provided.*

# ⑥ Planning and organising your writing

## Aim
- Learning to effectively plan and organise ideas, presenting complex information clearly.

## Lesson learning objectives
- Plan and organise your ideas, present complex information clearly, making meaning clear by using subject and verb agreement accurately.

## Lesson starter

Share the relevant aspect of the coverage and range with the students and go through the five steps on page 82 with them. Inform students that individually they will write a 500 word magazine article and discuss with them the word limit, and how tasks are often set with parameters. Direct them to the *Top tip* on page 82.

In preparation for the main activity, the students decide from reading the task (Task 1 of Activity 1) what information is provided that they as writers have been given to complete it. Set this information out as bullet points and share with the rest of the class in discussion.

## Main teaching

Pairs complete task 2 from page 82 of the student book, then feed back in class discussion. Remind students of the previous lessons and ensure that they understand the features of an article, the audience and purpose. They can use pages 60—68 as a resource if necessary. Students then go on individually to complete Tasks 2–5.

Students look at the checklist for subject-verb agreement on page 84 of the student book. Draw their attention to the need for technical accuracy, as stated in the standards. Pairs then complete Activities 1–4 on pages 84–85, feeding back to the class at the end of each. Also in pairs, they should discuss the advantages and disadvantages of planning, and consider any ideas for better planning/organisation.

## Plenary

Class feedback: draw out from students the drafting process of writing an article and the importance/benefits of planning responses before writing a first draft. Emphasise that this process is useful in real life.

## Homework

Students complete their draft of the magazine article from the lesson starter, making any other changes in light of what has been learned during the lesson.

## Answers

### Activity 1
1. a  Sentence A: one agent (the form of the verb is **incorrect**)

   Sentence B: many agents (the form of the verb is **correct**)

   Sentence C: one agent (the form of the verb is **incorrect**)

   Sentence D: many agents (the form of the verb is **incorrect**)

   Sentence E: one agent (the form of the verb is **correct**)

   b  A  If a person **wants** to find out what qualifications…

   C  Answering the career values questionnaire **helps** people work out…

   D  There's even a forum where site visitors **chat** about different issues.

### Activity 2
1. Go; need; wants; want; is

2. Go = one agent (you)

   need = one agent (you)

   wants = one agent (Amy)

   want = one agent (you)

   is = one agent (website)

Student book pages 86–89

# 7 Writing a briefing paper

## Aim

- Researching and understanding the basic structure, and purpose, of a briefing paper. Using apostrophes correctly.

## Lesson learning objectives

- Research and write a briefing paper, and make meaning clear by using apostrophes correctly.

## Lesson starter

Take students through the introduction and guidance on page 86 of the student book. Direct students to look at the four headings, which may be used to structure a report: issue, background, considerations and conclusion.

Ask students to look at Activity 1. Read the briefing paper on page 87 and identify the features used as outlined in the guidance. Feed back as a class.

## Main teaching and learning

Ask students to read Task 1b, and discuss how features used would help the intended audience understand the issue.

Direct students to look at the headings and discuss what they suggest about the information in each section. Ask students to consider the following questions:

Are there any headings that could be changed? What else, for example, might we use instead of 'pros' and 'cons'?

Discuss the questions as a class. Ask students to decide if the briefing paper is effective in the intended purpose of providing information that could lead to a decision being made.

Read the task and unpack it in terms of what is required. For feedback, invite volunteers to write the task out in bullets to share with the larger group.

Take students through the work on apostrophes on page 89. Individually complete Tasks 1 and 2 on the same page.

Swap draft with partner and check the use of apostrophes.

## Plenary

In pairs, discuss the successful features of the briefing papers and how effective they are in fulfilling the purpose.

## Homework

Write a final draft of the briefing paper.

# Answers

Activity 1 and Activity 2 are open student writing tasks, for which answers have not been supplied.

**Apostrophe activities**

1  b  The boy's red football shirts were dumped in the school's washing machine. They stained the lab technicians' white lab-coats pink.

2  If students don't have checklists they can't revise how to write each form.

# ⑧ Making a convincing argument

## Aim

- Effectively building clear arguments and backing up ideas/opinions with evidence.

## Lesson learning objectives

- Plan how to back up your ideas with evidence, build your argument and ensure your meaning is clear by using inverted commas correctly.

## Lesson starter

Share the relevant section of the coverage and range from the standards. Take students through the introductory paragraph on page 90 of the student book and ask them to consider what elements are required for building a structured argument. Terms, such as plan, evidence, supporting viewpoint and consideration of counter-argument could be integral here, as well as the PEEL plan (as on page 79 of the student book).

Read the *Top tip* and then Task 1 together as a class. Then students list points for and against this argument. Remind students about the importance of considering purpose, audience and form, and of the value of being able to understand an opposing viewpoint. Feed back as a class.

## Main teaching and learning

Students consider the advantages and disadvantages of advertising, listing them and then sharing their ideas with a partner before moving on to complete Task 4. They then look at evidence and examples and note some ideas. Direct students to look at the arguments for and against on page 91 of the student book.

Students now group and number points as instructed in Task 5 so that the argument is planned. End this activity by putting students in groups to share and discuss ideas.

Remind students of the PEEL plan from a previous lesson. They co-write a PEEL paragraph and feed back to the class. They then go back to their own plan and add more details, using what has been learned in writing the PEEL paragraph.

Move on to page 93 of the student book, and take students through the examples of how and when to use inverted commas. Provide a photocopy of Molly's text from Activity 1 so students can correct in pairs, annotating and highlighting as necessary. Students then complete Task 2, individually writing an article and using inverted commas where appropriate.

## Plenary

Feed back about the articles written by the students, using the 'checklist' from Task 2b and discussing any points emerging from the peer assessments.

## Homework

Students practise their skills by writing the article as instructed from Task 2 on page 93. (Provide an alternative task for students, if necessary e.g. should we ban smoking for all parents?)

## Answers

### Activity 1–3

*These activities are open student writing activities, for which answers have not been supplied.*

**Clear meaning – Activity 1**

1  Check inverted commas have been properly used.

2  This is another open student writing activity.

# ⑨ Writing a report

## Aim

- Writing clear reports, concise in meaning and accurate, with correct spelling and grammar.

## Lesson learning objectives

- Write a report; use verbs in correct tenses so that meaning is clear; ensure meaning is clear by improving your spelling; check your work to ensure it is clear and accurate.

## Lesson starter

Ask students to discuss:
1  what they think is a report
2  how they think a report should be presented
3  the purpose of a report – real-life purpose.

Draw attention to the guidance and the *Top tip* on page 94 of the student book.

Ask students to discuss the differences between a report and a news report. Feed back to the class.

## Main teaching and learning

Students read the report on page 95 and complete Activity 1. A photocopy of the text could be given to them, or they can highlight features, or they could list them on a flip chart. When they are finished, discuss their answers as a class.

Move on to page 96 and look at Activity 2 together. Students complete Tasks 1 and 2, then 3–5 individually. The final task asks to write a first draft of their report.

Take the class through the guidance on verb tenses on page 97 of the student book, before students complete Activity 1 on the same page. Feed back to the class.

Then, in small groups, look at 'Learn to spell a new word' on page 98. Ask each group to make up a rule to avoid incorrect uses of homophones and share the rule with the class. Students then complete Activity 2.

If there is time left in the lesson, move on to page 99 of the student book. Students read through the guidance on checking their work, then complete Activity 3.

## Plenary

Discuss with students what has worked well and which areas need more work.

## Homework

Students write final draft of their report from the last activity, using what they have learned from this lesson.

# Introduction to the Edexcel sample assessment material

In this section you will find a description of exactly how students should be assessed for each area. This is followed by a sample assessment paper and mark schemes; sample student answers and examiner commentary have been provided for this paper, to illustrate a selection of pass and fail answers. Finally, there is an additional practice assessment paper (including Reading, Writing and SLC) for students to try.

## The assessments

At Level 2, students need to complete two assessments at designated times in which they *make a range of contributions to discussions in a range of contexts, including those that are unfamiliar, and make effective presentations.* There are two key features required at Level 2: students make presentations in addition to participation in discussion and they must also demonstrate that they are able to cope with unfamiliar contexts/situations.

The order in which the formal assessment takes place is at the discretion of the centre and again, the emphasis is on a formal assessment, rather than an 'opportunistic' approach. In the completion of the assessment record sheet, any unfamiliar situations need to be identified.

Students are expected to:
- consider complex information and give a relevant, cogent response in appropriate language
- present information and ideas clearly and persuasively to others
- adapt contributions to suit audience, purpose and situation
- make significant contributions to discussions, taking a range of roles and helping to move discussion forward.

## Discussion activity

Usually a maximum number of five students would make up the discussion, although not all those involved need to be assessed. All those being assessed must have sufficient opportunity to contribute to the discussion. An assessor may prompt discussions if necessary, which should be noted. At no time should an assessor be an active participant.

## Presentation activity

Learners may deliver presentations individually or as part of a small group. If the presentation is delivered in a small group, each individual learner's contribution must be sufficiently developed to demonstrate functionality at Level 2. Learners must ensure that their preparation and their part of the presentation is all their own work.

---

### Example activity ideas : Discussion

**Context**

Centres should devise their own activities. The following examples may be helpful as ideas or to adapt.
- a planning meeting to arrange a visit from a local business in the community (among peers)
- a discussion with an external visitor for example about local issues, vocational information
- a decision-making exercise for example through a committee or debate

---

### Example activity ideas : Presentation

**Context**

Centres should devise their own activities. The following examples may be helpful as ideas or to adapt.
- persuade audience of a current concern such as a health and safety issue
- a persuasive sales pitch for a new product
- persuade audience of a particular viewpoint on a topical issue, e.g. the case for free school dinners.

---

All contexts may be adapted to suit a presentation or formal discussion and to include an unfamiliar element (which must be assessed at least once). The unfamiliar element may arise from either the subject/topic or the audience/group (for example a different tutor group or an external visitor).

## How was the discussion organised?

This would include information such as the presence of any outside visitors, the use of support/prompt sheets to assist the activity, the number of people involved in the discussion and the contribution of the assessor.

## How was the presentation organised?

This would include information such as any uses of electronic delivery, use of resources, the length of presentation and the subsequent follow-up e.g. question and answer session.

Any learner support?

This may include:
- prior preparation
- notes/research
- examples to describe the unfamiliarity of the context/audience/activity
- logistics/organisation of assessment activity.

# How students will be assessed – Reading

Your students' reading is assessed in one 45-minute exam. The total number of marks for the reading paper is 25.

The reading paper is divided into three sections, A, B and C. Each section has a text to read and questions to answer about it. Each question states the number of marks it is worth. All three texts are on the same subject or theme. You will be given space to write your answers.

The table below shows the types of question students will be asked and what they should do in each case.

| Types of question | What students should do |
|---|---|
| Identify the main purpose of the text | Give a short written answer. |
| Multiple choice | Select the correct option to complete an unfinished sentence or to answer a question. Put a cross in a box to show their answer. |
| Find a number of pieces of information and evidence in the text | Give short written answers. |
| Decide whether statements they are given are presented in the text as facts or opinions | Place a tick in the correct column for each statement. |
| Give features of the text that convey information – for example, headings, lists | Give short written answers. |
| Respond to the text – find the solutions to questions by using information in the text | Write their own views based on information from the text. There will be a number of possible answers. |
| Make a decision based on comparing information in different parts of the text. | Written answer. There will be no right answer, but they will need to give three reasons for their decision. Their answer and reasons must be based on information in the text. |

# How students will be assessed – Speaking, listening and communication

You will assess your students' speaking, listening and communication skills. They may take time ahead of their assessments to research and prepare what they want to say and they can use notes to help them on the day. They can use visual aids, if they wish.

The table below shows the tasks students will have to complete and what they should do in each case.

| Type of task | Who with? | Time | Students must show that they can |
|---|---|---|---|
| Discussion | About four others | About 20 minutes | Respond to information in a way that is relevant and understandable.<br><br>Make contributions to the discussion using appropriate language.<br><br>Take a range of roles – listening, chairing, speaking, responding, etc.<br><br>Help to move the discussion forward by asking questions, summarising, etc. |
| Presentation | On their own or as part of a small group | About 10 minutes | Present their ideas clearly.<br><br>Use appropriate language.<br><br>Speak persuasively.<br><br>Speak appropriately for different audiences, purposes and situations. |

# How students will be assessed – Writing

Students' writing is assessed in one 45-minute exam. There are two tasks which assess their writing skills. The total number of marks for the Writing paper is 25.

For each task, students will be given some information. They will then be given a writing task based on it. They will be told what form to write in, and they may be given some guidance on what to include.

The table below shows what students will be assessed on and what they must show they can do.

| What students will be assessed on | They must show that they can |
|---|---|
| Form, communication and purpose | Use the correct format for writing. For example, a report with headings. |
| | Organise their writing, using paragraphs and other features such as headings if needed. |
| | Include all the relevant information the reader needs, and present it clearly so that they can understand it. |
| | Write persuasively if asked to. |
| | Use appropriate language for the purpose. |
| | Write to meet the purpose. For example, to persuade or to inform. |
| Spelling, punctuation and grammar | Ensure spelling and grammar are accurate and the reader can understand their meaning |
| | Use a range of punctuation correctly. |

# Reading

Edexcel Functional Skills

# Functional English

## Level 2: Reading

| Sample Assessment Material<br>Time: 45 minutes | Paper Reference(s)<br>**XXXX/XX** |
|---|---|
| **You may use a dictionary.**<br>**You do not need to write in complete sentences.** | Total Marks<br>**25** |

## Instructions

- Use **black** ink or ball-point pen.
- **Fill in the boxes** at the top of this page with your name, centre number and candidate number.
- Answer **all** questions.
- Answer the questions in the spaces provided.
  - *There may be more space than you need.*
- Dictionaries may be used.

## Information

- The total mark for this paper is 25.
- The marks for **each** question are shown in brackets.
  - *Use this as a guide as to how much time to spend on each question.*

## Advice

- Read each question carefully before you start to answer it.
- Keep an eye on the time.
- Try to answer every question.
- Check your answers if you have time at the end.

*Turn over* ▶

**SECTION A**

Read Text A and answer questions 1–6.

**Text A**

You have recently passed your driving test, and have found this article while searching for information about driving on the internet.

## Telegraph.co.uk

By John Bingham

# Motorists back 'etiquette'* section for driving test

**The driving test should be overhauled to include a new 'etiquette' section to tackle road rage, middle lane hogging and selfish parking, a poll has found.**

Four out of five motorists would back the idea if it helped curb 'sins' such as overtaking on the inside or bad parking, the poll found.

There was also strong support for making all drivers retake their tests periodically to iron out bad habits.

Overall, 82 per cent supported the idea of adding a motoring etiquette section to driving tests, according to the poll carried out for Intune, the car insurer.

Those who take up more than one space in the car park or cut other motorists up on the road caused most annoyance, each identified by 80 per cent of respondents as the most irritating traits in other motorists.

Road rage and hogging the middle lane of the motorway were also near the top of the list of bad habits, singled out by 77 per cent and 75 per cent of respondents respectively.

Meanwhile two thirds said they would back a change in the law to force all motorists to retake their test regularly, while four out of five said those over 70 should be made to do so.

"Statistically, older drivers have more accidents but they are more likely to be minor accidents," said Mark Gettinby, director of financial services at Intune.

"Taking the time to be polite towards other road users will also help make the roads safer for everyone."

GfK NOP polled just under 1,000 drivers for the survey.

*etiquette – good manners/politeness

**1** What is the main purpose of Text A?

...................................................................................................................................................................

(1 mark)

**Answer questions 2 to 3 with a cross in the box ☒. If you change your mind about an answer, put a line through the box ☒ and then mark your new answer with a cross ☒.**

**2** What percentage of the drivers polled would support the addition of an etiquette section to the driving test?

A ☐ 70 per cent

B ☐ 75 per cent

C ☐ 82 per cent

D ☐ 77 per cent

(1 mark)

**3** Mark Gettinby states that older drivers:

A ☐ are likely to have more serious accidents

B ☐ are likely to have fewer serious accidents

C ☐ are likely to want more re-testing

D ☐ are likely to be more polite

(1 mark)

**4** Identify **two** changes that are recommended for the driving test, according to Text A.

You do **not** need to write in sentences.

i) ................................................................................................................

................................................................................................................

ii) ................................................................................................................

................................................................................................................

(2 marks)

**5** Place a tick in the correct column for **each** of the six statements to show which are presented in the article as facts and which are opinions.

| | Fact | Opinion |
|---|---|---|
| Bad habits will end if etiquette is part of the driving test. | | |
| Two thirds of those surveyed back motorists retaking the driving test. | | |
| Repeated driving tests will solve all the problems. | | |
| Motorists are annoyed about being cut up on the road by other drivers. | | |
| Most drivers support including etiquette in the driving test. | | |
| Good etiquette will lead to much safer roads. | | |

(3 marks)

**6** Text A claims that 'Motorists back "etiquette" section for driving test'.

From your reading of the information provided, give **two** reasons why this text might be biased.

You do **not** need to write in sentences.

i) ......................................................................................................................................

......................................................................................................................................

ii) ......................................................................................................................................

......................................................................................................................................

(2 marks)

**TOTAL FOR SECTION A = 10 MARKS**

## SECTION B

Read Text B and answer questions 7–11.

**Text B**

As a new driver you have been researching satnavs. You have found this information on 'Think!', the Department for Transport road safety website.

**Road Safety**

### Satellite navigation (satnav)

Here are some frequently asked questions and answers about satnav.

**Where should my satnav be fitted?**

Fix items where they are legal and don't interfere with safety. It is an offence to drive without proper control of the vehicle and full view of the road and traffic ahead. A vehicle could fail its MOT if a device is installed where driver vision is affected.

Items should be fixed in a safe position away from airbag covers and areas where they might cause injury in the event of a crash. Always read the instructions for the satnav device and follow any manufacturer installation instructions. Vehicle manufacturers may also have advice on how best to install devices.

**I need to change my destination location, what should I do?**

You must always exercise proper control of the vehicle. The Highway Code (Rule 150) warns drivers not to be distracted by in-vehicle systems. You should enter information into your satnav only when you have found a safe place to stop.

**Should I always trust and follow the satnav directions?**

As a driver you are responsible for the route you take; do not blindly follow directions from any satnav. You must take into account road conditions, road works and obey statutory road signs.

**7** What it the main purpose of Text B?

.......................................................................................................................................................

(1 mark)

**8** Give **three** features of Text B that help to convey information.

You do **not** need to write in sentences.

i) .............................................................................................................................................

.............................................................................................................................................

ii) ...........................................................................................................................................

.............................................................................................................................................

iii) ..........................................................................................................................................

.............................................................................................................................................

(3 marks)

**9** Apart from your satnav, give two examples from Text B of what you must take into consideration when driving safely.

You do **not** need to write in sentences.

i) .............................................................................................................................................

.............................................................................................................................................

ii) ...........................................................................................................................................

.............................................................................................................................................

(2 marks)

**10** According to Text B, what should you do if you want to enter information into your satnav?

................................................................................................................................................

(1 mark)

**11** Your friend is considering buying a satnav. Which **three** aspects from Text B do you think are the most important for them to understand?

You do **not** need to write in sentences.

i) ................................................................................................................................................

................................................................................................................................................

ii) ................................................................................................................................................

................................................................................................................................................

iii) ................................................................................................................................................

................................................................................................................................................

(3 marks)

**TOTAL FOR SECTION B = 10 MARKS**

## SECTION C

Read Text C and answer questions 12–14.

**Text C**

You have found three adverts for second hand cars.

Ford Fiesta 1.3 Encore
1998 (S reg), 82,000 miles, manual gearbox, 3 previous owners, road tax paid for 6 months

Metallic Blue, 5 door, hatchback
Radio/Cassette

Immobiliser and factory-fitted car alarm, child locks on rear doors, driver and passenger airbags.

**Advert 1** – Local shop window

**£599**

**Car for sale – contact 07895126466**

**Advert 2** – Classified Adverts in Newspaper

**1994 (M reg) Ford Fiesta**
1.3 Equipe, Special Edition,
83,000 miles, Automatic gearbox,
Blue, 3 door, hatchback,
11 months road tax paid,
two previous owners, new Sony XMP3
Stereo with Bluetooth fitted.
£500 only. 07771455271.

**Advert 3** – Online

www.usedcarsforsale.co.uk

**Used Ford Fiesta 1.2 Zetec, 1996 (N reg), manual gearbox, Silver, 24000 miles, 3 door, hatchback, CD Player, Sun roof.**
One owner from new. Good condition.
Currently untaxed.
**£500 - Contact Seller on 07771234568.**

**12** Your friend is looking for a car with a manual gearbox and has a budget of £500. Which of the three cars in Text C would you recommend?

Remember to give the number of the advert in your answer.

You do **not** need to write in sentences.

......................................................................................................................................................

(1 mark)

**13** A member of your family would also like a car. She would like a car with good safety features. Which of the three cars in Text C would you recommend?

Remember to give the number of the advert in your answer.

You do **not** need to write in sentences.

......................................................................................................................................................

(1 mark)

**14** Consider the information provided in the three adverts in Text C. Based on this information which car would you choose to go and look at?

Give **three** reasons.

Remember to give the number of the advert in your answer.

You do **not** need to write in sentences.

Car chosen ......................................................................................................................................

Reason i)  ........................................................................................................................................

Reason ii)  .......................................................................................................................................

Reason iii)  ......................................................................................................................................

(3 marks)

**TOTAL FOR SECTION C = 5 MARKS**

**TOTAL FOR PAPER = 25 MARKS**

# Mark scheme: Reading

## Section A

| Question Number | Answer | Mark |
|---|---|---|
| 1 | To persuade the reader that motorists back the addition of etiquette to the driving test. (1)<br><br>Accept any reasonable answer based on the text. | (1) |

| Question Number | Answer | Mark |
|---|---|---|
| 2 | C – 82 per cent | (1) |

| Question Number | Answer | Mark |
|---|---|---|
| 3 | B – are likely to have fewer serious accidents | (1) |

| Question Number | Answer | Mark |
|---|---|---|
| 4 | • add etiquette to the driving test (1)<br>• all drivers to re-take tests regularly (1)<br>• drivers over 70 re-take their test (1)<br><br>One mark for each correct answer, up to a maximum of **two** marks. | (2) |

| Question Number | Answer | Mark |
|---|---|---|
| 5 | | | |

|  | Fact | Opinion |
|---|---|---|
| Bad habits will end if etiquette is part of the driving test. |  | ✓ |
| Two thirds of those surveyed back motorists re-taking the driving test. | ✓ |  |
| Repeated driving tests will solve all the problems. |  | ✓ |
| Motorists are annoyed about being cut up on the road by other drivers. | ✓ |  |
| Most drivers support including etiquette in driving test. | ✓ |  |
| Good etiquette will lead to much safer roads. |  | ✓ |

**For 0 or 1 correct – 0 marks**
**For 2 or 3 correct - 1 mark**
**For 4 or 5 correct – 2 marks**
**For 6 correct – 3 marks**

(3)

| Question Number | Answer | Mark |
|---|---|---|
| 6 | Answers may include:<br>• exaggeration (1)<br>• only based on a small sample of drivers (1)<br>• doesn't give other side of the argument/one-sided view (1)<br>• persuasive language used, e.g. sins, strong support. (1)<br><br>Accept any reasonable answer, based on the text, up to a maximum of **two** marks. | (2) |

**Section B**

| Question Number | Answer | Mark |
|---|---|---|
| 7 | To inform drivers about using satnav (safely). (1) | |
| | Accept any reasonable answer based on the text. | (1) |

| Question Number | Answer | Mark |
|---|---|---|
| 8 | Answers may include: | |
| | • question and answer style/FAQs make the information clear (1) | |
| | • use of bold makes questions stand out/easy to locate (1) | |
| | • logo shows it is official – can trust the information (1) | |
| | • uses references to the Highway Code to support information. (1) | |
| | Accept any reasonable answer, based on the text, up to a maximum of **three** marks. | (3) |

| Question Number | Answer | Mark |
|---|---|---|
| 9 | • road conditions (1) | |
| | • road works (1) | |
| | • statutory road signs (1) | |
| | One mark for each correct answer up to a maximum of **two marks**. | (2) |

| Question Number | Answer | Mark |
|---|---|---|
| 10 | Make sure you have stopped your vehicle in a safe place. (1) | |
| | Accept any reasonable answer based on the text. | (1) |

| Question Number | Answer | Mark |
|---|---|---|
| 11 | Answers may include: | |
| | • fit in a safe position away from airbag covers (1) | |
| | • fit where driver vision is not affected (1) | |
| | • fit where they are legal (1) | |
| | • fit where they don't interfere with safety (1) | |
| | • fit using manufacturing instructions. (1) | |
| | Accept any reasonable answer, based on the text, up to a maximum of **three** marks. | (3) |

| Question Number | Answer | Mark |
|---|---|---|
| 12 | Car three/Advert three (Ford Fiesta 1.2 Zetec) | (1) |

| Question Number | Answer | Mark |
|---|---|---|
| 13 | Car one/Advert one (Ford Fiesta 1.3 Encore) | (1) |

| Question Number | Answer | Mark |
|---|---|---|
| **15** | Any car may be chosen.<br>Reasons may include:<br>• age<br>• owners<br>• tax<br>• mileage<br>• colour/finish<br>• price. | |
| | Accept any reasonable answer, based on the text, up to a maximum of **three** marks. | (3) |

# Writing

Edexcel Functional Skills

# Functional English

## Level 2: Writing

| | |
|---|---|
| **Sample Assessment Material**<br>**Time: 45 minutes** | Paper Reference(s)<br>**XXXX/XX** |
| **You may use a dictionary.**<br>**You do not need to write in complete sentences.** | Total Marks<br>**25** |

## Instructions

- Use **black** ink or ball-point pen.
- **Fill in the boxes** at the top of this page with your name, centre number and candidate number.
- Answer **both** questions.
- Answer the questions in the spaces provided.
  - *There may be more space than you need.*
- Dictionaries may be used.

## Information

- The total mark for this paper is 25.
- The marks for **each** question are shown in brackets.
  - *Use this as a guide as to how much time to spend on each question.*
- You will be assessed on spelling, punctuation and grammar in both tasks.

## Advice

- Read each question carefully before you start to answer it.
- Keep an eye on the time.
- Try to answer every question.
- Check your answers if you have time at the end.

*Turn over* ▶

There are **two** tasks which assess your writing skills.

Remember that spelling, punctuation and grammar will be assessed in **both** tasks.

**Task 1**

**Information**

Your school/college/workplace has asked for ideas about a charitable project to support. You have found this information about mobile phone recycling.

### The Phone Shop Mobile Phone Recycling Scheme

**Recycle your phone – to help the environment and to help local charities.**

Recycling is easy to do, great for the environment and won't cost you a penny.

The Phone Shop has teamed up with Charitable Mobile Recycling (CMR) to launch a simple scheme that raises money for charity from unwanted mobile phones. This also prevents mobile phones going to landfill sites. For every 200 phones recycled we will donate £300 to local charities.

**Mobile phone facts**
*   The average mobile phone user will replace their handset once every 18 months.
*   Less than 20% of all unused mobile phones in the UK are currently recycled.
*   Latest figures suggest close to 90 million phones are never used. If you put 90 million phones end to end, they would stretch from Lands End to John O'Groats and back OVER THREE TIMES.
*   Mobile phones contain toxic substances which need to be disposed of in a safe manner. If these end up in landfill sites they become a threat to human health and the environment.

**How do I recycle my mobile phone?**

First you need to register for the scheme at our website www.thephoneshop/Recycling

Collection boxes are available if you are collecting 20 phones or more. Just order a collection box when you register and when it is full arrange a FREE collection through our website. This is ideal for an office, college or school collection.

You can recycle mobile phones of any brand and in any condition. Every phone can make a difference.

**Writing task**

Write a briefing paper about this scheme to help your school/college/workplace make its decision.

In your briefing paper, you may include:
*   background information about the scheme
*   the advantages and disadvantages of running this scheme at your school/college/workplace
*   whether or not you recommend this scheme.

(15 marks)

.....................................................................................................................
.....................................................................................................................
.....................................................................................................................
.....................................................................................................................
.....................................................................................................................
.....................................................................................................................
.....................................................................................................................
.....................................................................................................................
.....................................................................................................................
.....................................................................................................................
.....................................................................................................................
.....................................................................................................................
.....................................................................................................................
.....................................................................................................................
.....................................................................................................................
.....................................................................................................................
.....................................................................................................................
.....................................................................................................................
.....................................................................................................................
.....................................................................................................................
.....................................................................................................................
.....................................................................................................................
.....................................................................................................................
.....................................................................................................................
.....................................................................................................................
.....................................................................................................................
.....................................................................................................................
.....................................................................................................................
.....................................................................................................................

**TOTAL FOR TASK 1 = 15 MARKS**

**Task 2**

**Information**

You live in Rook Lane and have received this information sheet.

# Estrick County Council Notice to Residents

## Access arrangements for forthcoming Fun Fair

The fun fair is coming to Estrick Park in the centre of the town from July 7th–July 11th.

Cycle paths across the park will be closed during this period.

Car parking for visitors will be made available in the following roads: Banks Lane, Douglas Street, Chandlers Road and Market Street.

Temporary toilets will be placed in Rook Lane. Rook Lane will be closed to traffic. Residents should make alternative arrangements for parking.

If you wish to comment on any of these arrangements, please contact Cathy Oldman at Estrick County Council.

Email: c.oldman@estrickcc.gov.uk

**Writing task**

You are very unhappy about the arrangements for the fun fair.

Write an email to Cathy Oldman at Estrick County Council, protesting against the arrangements.

(10 marks)

**Begin your answer on the next page.**

| New Message |
| --- |
| **From:** you@your.email.co.uk |
| **To:** c.oldman@estrickcc.gov.uk |
| **Subject:** Fun Fair arrangements |

..............................................................................................................................
..............................................................................................................................
..............................................................................................................................
..............................................................................................................................
..............................................................................................................................
..............................................................................................................................
..............................................................................................................................
..............................................................................................................................
..............................................................................................................................
..............................................................................................................................
..............................................................................................................................
..............................................................................................................................
..............................................................................................................................
..............................................................................................................................
..............................................................................................................................
..............................................................................................................................
..............................................................................................................................
..............................................................................................................................
..............................................................................................................................
..............................................................................................................................
..............................................................................................................................
..............................................................................................................................
..............................................................................................................................
..............................................................................................................................
..............................................................................................................................

........................................................................................

........................................................................................

........................................................................................

........................................................................................

........................................................................................

........................................................................................

........................................................................................

........................................................................................

........................................................................................

........................................................................................

........................................................................................

........................................................................................

........................................................................................

........................................................................................

........................................................................................

........................................................................................

........................................................................................

........................................................................................

........................................................................................

........................................................................................

........................................................................................

........................................................................................

........................................................................................

........................................................................................

........................................................................................

........................................................................................

........................................................................................

........................................................................................

........................................................................................

........................................................................................

**TOTAL FOR TASK 2 = 10 MARKS**

**TOTAL FOR PAPER = 25 MARKS**

# Mark scheme: Writing

| Task | | |
|------|--|--|
| **1** | | Write a briefing paper about this scheme to help your school/college/workplace make its decision. In your briefing paper, you may include:<br>• background information about the scheme<br>• the advantages and disadvantages of running this scheme at your school/college/workplace<br>• whether or not you recommend this scheme.<br><div align="right">**(15 marks)**</div> |
| | **Indicative content** | |
| | | • Uses appropriate tone/language when writing the briefing paper.<br>• Some detail regarding the content of the briefing paper and its purpose.<br>• Some explanation of the project scheme and the advantages of recycling mobile phones.<br>• The advantages and disadvantages of the school/college/workplace running the scheme e.g. how easily it could be publicised/organised, appropriate central location for the collection box.<br>• Reasons given on whether or not would recommend the scheme. |

| Mark | A: Form, communication and purpose |
|------|-----------------------------------|
| 0 | No rewardable material. |
| 1–3 | • Presents relevant information/ideas logically to a limited extent.<br>• Basic ability to present complex ideas/information evident.<br>• Uses language for specific purpose to a limited extent.<br>• Uses a limited range of sentence structures with limited accuracy.<br>• Makes limited use of paragraphing and other organisational features with basic accuracy. |
| 4–6 | • Presents relevant information/ideas logically for some of the response.<br>• Able to present complex ideas/information clearly and concisely with some lapses.<br>• Uses language for specific purpose for some of the response.<br>• Uses a range of sentence structures with some accuracy.<br>• Makes some use of paragraphing and other organisational features with some accuracy. |
| 7–9 | • Presents relevant information/ideas logically for most of the response.<br>• Able to present complex ideas/information clearly and concisely, with occasional lapses.<br>• Uses language for specific purpose throughout the response.<br>• Uses a range of sentence structures accurately.<br>• Makes consistent use of appropriate paragraphing and other organisational features with accuracy. |

| Mark | B: Spelling, punctuation and grammar |
|------|--------------------------------------|
| 0 | No rewardable material. |
| 1–2 | • Uses spelling and grammar with limited accuracy, supporting meaning at a basic level.<br>• Uses basic punctuation e.g. commas, apostrophes and inverted commas with limited accuracy. |
| 3–4 | • Uses spelling and grammar with some accuracy, supporting meaning some of the time.<br>• Uses some punctuation e.g. commas, apostrophes and inverted commas correctly and appropriately. |
| 5–6 | • Use of spelling and grammar is mostly accurate, supporting meaning most of the time.<br>• Uses a range of punctuation e.g. commas, apostrophes and inverted commas correctly and appropriately most of the time. |

| Task | | |
|---|---|---|
| 2 | You are very unhappy about the arrangements for the fun fair. | |
| | Write an email to Cathy Oldman at Estrick County Council, protesting against the arrangements. | |
| | | **(10 marks)** |
| | **Indicative content** | |
| | • Uses relevant organisational features.<br>• Uses appropriate tone/language when writing a complaint/protest email about the fun fair arrangements.<br>• Shows awareness of audience. | |

| Mark | A: Form, communication and purpose |
|---|---|
| 0 | No rewardable material. |
| 1–2 | • Presents relevant information/ideas logically, using persuasive language as appropriate, to a limited extent.<br>• Basic ability to present complex ideas/information evident.<br>• Uses language for the specific purpose, to a limited extent.<br>• Makes use of a limited range of sentence structures with limited accuracy.<br>• Makes limited use of paragraphing and other organisational features with basic accuracy. |
| 3–4 | • Presents relevant information/ideas logically, using persuasive language as appropriate, for some of the response.<br>• Able to present complex ideas/information clearly and concisely with some lapses.<br>• Uses language for the specific purpose, for some of the response.<br>• Uses a range of sentence structures with some accuracy.<br>• Makes some use of paragraphing and other organisational features with some accuracy. |
| 5–6 | • Presents relevant information/ideas logically, using persuasive language as appropriate, for most of the response.<br>• Able to present complex ideas/information clearly and concisely with occasional lapses.<br>• Uses language for the specific purpose, throughout the response.<br>• Uses a range of sentence structures accurately.<br>• Makes consistent use of appropriate paragraphing and other organisational features. |

| Mark | B: Spelling, punctuation and grammar |
|---|---|
| 0 | No rewardable material. |
| 1–2 | • Uses spelling and grammar with limited accuracy, supporting meaning at a basic level.<br>• Uses basic punctuation e.g. commas, apostrophes and inverted commas with limited accuracy. |
| 3–4 | • Use of spelling and grammar is mostly accurate, supporting meaning most of the time.<br>• Uses some punctuation e.g. commas, apostrophes and inverted commas correctly and appropriately most of the time. |

# Sample Reading answers – pass

## Reading Level 2 pass answer

**1** What is the main purpose of Text A?

To persuade people that motorists are in favour of adding etiquette to the driving test

(1 mark)

This is correct because Text A is a news report claiming that a poll of motorists shows that 'four out of five' would back this idea.

**Answer questions 2 to 3 with a cross in the box ⊠. If you change your mind about an answer, put a line through the box ⊠ and then mark your new answer with a cross ⊠.**

**2** What percentage of the drivers polled would support the addition of an etiquette section to the driving test?

A ☐ 70 per cent

B ☐ 75 per cent

C ⊠ 82 per cent

D ☐ 77 per cent

This is correct because 'Overall, 82 per cent supported the idea.'

(1 mark)

**3** Mark Gettinby states that older drivers:

A ☐ are likely to have more serious accidents

B ⊠ are likely to have fewer serious accidents

C ☐ are likely to want more re-testing

D ☐ are likely to be more polite

This is correct because Mark Gettinby states that accidents involving older drivers 'are more likely to be minor accidents'.

(1 mark)

# Sample Reading answers – pass

**4** Identify **two** changes that are recommended for the driving test, according to Text A.

You do **not** need to write in sentences.

i) to retake the driving test regularly

ii) people over 70 should retake their test again

> These are both correct because the text reports that two thirds of motorists would back i) and four out of five would back ii).

(2 marks)

**5** Place a tick in the correct column for **each** of the six statements to show which are presented in the article as facts and which are opinions.

| | Fact | Opinion |
|---|---|---|
| Bad habits will end if etiquette is part of the driving test. | | ✓ |
| Two thirds of those surveyed back motorists retaking the driving test. | ✓ | |
| Repeated driving tests will solve all the problems. | | ✓ |
| Motorists are annoyed about being cut up on the road by other drivers. | ✓ | |
| Most drivers support including etiquette in the driving test. | ✓ | |
| Good etiquette will lead to much safer roads. | | ✓ |

(3 marks)

> These are all facts because evidence is provided by the survey of motorists to support them.

> These are all opinions because there is no evidence to support that these outcomes will actually result from what is suggested.

# Sample Reading answers – pass

**6** Text A claims that 'Motorists back 'etiquette' section for driving test'.

From your reading of the information provided, give **two** reasons why this text might be biased.

You do **not** need to write in sentences.

i) the text is biased because it only focused on bad habits on the road ......

ii) not many (under 1,000) people in the survey ......

(2 marks)

> The first reason suggests that the survey gives only one side of the argument and the second that it might not represent the views of motorists generally because too few people were surveyed. Both of these are valid suggestions that the text might be biased.

**TOTAL FOR SECTION A = 10 MARKS**

# Sample Reading answers – pass

**7** What it the main purpose of Text B?

To give people tips on satnavs such as where to place it, etc.

This is correct because Text B is a question and answer sheet giving information about using satnavs safely.

(1 mark)

**8** Give **three** features of Text B that help to convey information.

You do **not** need to write in sentences.

i) they use questions that people usually ask

ii) bold writing to make it stand out

iii) tells you which bit of the Highway Code it is

These are correct because they are all features that help to convey information.

(3 marks)

**9** Apart from your satnav, give two examples from Text B of what you must take into consideration when driving safely.

You do **not** need to write in sentences.

i) road condition

ii) road signs

Both of these are correct because the final sentence states 'You must take into account road conditions, road works and obey statutory road signs.'

(2 marks)

# Sample Reading answers – pass

**10** According to Text B, what should you do if you want to enter information into your satnav?

Stop at a safe place.

> This is correct because Text B says, 'You should enter information into your satnav only when you have found a safe place to stop.'

(1 mark)

**11** Your friend is considering buying a satnav. Which **three** aspects from Text B do you think are the most important for them to understand?

You do **not** need to write in sentences.

i) Always read the instructions for the satnav device and follow any manufacturer installation instructions.

ii) Don't block vision with satnav

iii) Don't place it in an unsafe position

> These are correct because they are all considerations mentioned in Text B that are important for satnav owners.

(3 marks)

**TOTAL FOR SECTION B = 10 MARKS**

# Sample Reading answers – pass

**12** Your friend is looking for a car with a manual gearbox and has a budget of £500. Which of the three cars in Text C would you recommend?

Remember to give the number of the advert in your answer.

You do **not** need to write in sentences.

*Car in Advert 3*

> This is correct because this car has a manual gearbox and costs £500.

(1 mark)

**13** A member of your family would also like a car. She would like a car with good safety features. Which of the three cars in Text C would you recommend?

Remember to give the number of the advert in your answer.

You do **not** need to write in sentences.

*Car in Advert 1*

> This is correct because this car has a number of safety features, such as an immobilizer, car alarm, child locks and airbags.

(1 mark)

**14** Consider the information provided in the three adverts in Text C. Based on this information which car would you choose to go and look at?

Give **three** reasons.

Remember to give the number of the advert in your answer.

You do **not** need to write in sentences.

Car chosen    *Car in Advert 1 because:*

Reason i)    *it's a newer car than the other two*

Reason ii)    *it's got good safety features*

Reason iii)    *road tax paid for 6 months*

> These are correct because they are all valid reasons for choosing the car in Advert 1.

(3 marks)

**TOTAL FOR SECTION C = 5 MARKS**

**TOTAL FOR PAPER = 25 MARKS**

# Sample Reading answers – fail

**1** What is the main purpose of Text A.

What motorists think about car drivers

This is incorrect because it doe[s] not show a purpose. When you answer a question asking for purpose, you should always beg[in] with 'to' – e.g. to persuade …, [to] inform … , to describe …, etc.

(1 mark)

**Answer questions 2 to 3 with a cross in the box ⊠. If you change your mind about an answer, put a line through the box ⊠ and then mark your new answer with a cross ⊠.**

**2** What percentage of the drivers polled would support the addition of an etiquette section to the driving test?

A ⊠ 70 per cent

B ⊠ 75 per cent

C ☐ 82 per cent

D ⊠ 77 per cent

This is incorrect because 70 per cent is not one of the statistics quoted in the text.

This is incorrect because 75 per cent is the figure given for the percentage of respondents who thought that hogging the middle lane of the motorway was a bad habit for drivers.

This is incorrect because 77 per cent is the figure given for the percentage of respondents who thought that road rage was a bad habit for drivers.

(1 mark)

**3** Mark Gettinby states that older drivers:

A ⊠ are likely to have more serious accidents

B ☐ are likely to have fewer serious accidents

C ⊠ are likely to want more re-testing

D ⊠ are likely to be more polite

This is incorrect because Mark Gettinby states that accidents involving older drivers 'are more likely to be minor accidents'.

This is incorrect because he does not mention re-testing.

This is incorrect because he does not say this about older drivers.

(1 mark)

# Sample Reading answers – fail

**4** Identify **two** changes that are recommended for the driving test, according to Text A.

You do **not** need to write in sentences.

i) drive politely .......................................................................................................

.......................................................................................................

ii) stop people overtaking on the inside .......................................................

.......................................................................................................

These are both incorrect because neither are recommendations made in Text A for changes to the driving test.

(2 marks)

**5** Place a tick in the correct column for **each** of the six statements to show which are presented in the article as facts and which are opinions.

|  | Fact | Opinion |
|---|---|---|
| Bad habits will end if etiquette is part of the driving test. | ✓ |  |
| Two thirds of those surveyed back motorists retaking the driving test. |  | ✓ |
| Repeated driving tests will solve all the problems. | ✓ |  |
| Motorists are annoyed about being cut up on the road by other drivers. |  | ✓ |
| Most drivers support including etiquette in the driving test. |  | ✓ |
| Good etiquette will lead to much safer roads. | ✓ |  |

(3 marks)

These are not facts because they are all beliefs that have not yet been tested. Therefore there is no evidence to support them.

These are not opinions because they can all be backed up by evidence from the GfK NOP poll.

# Sample Reading answers – fail

**6** Text A claims that 'Motorists back 'etiquette' section for driving test'.

From your reading of the information provided, give **two** reasons why this text might be biased.

You do **not** need to write in sentences.

i) some motorists are good drivers and have good etiquette

> The first answer is an opinion of the reader and does not stem from the information provided.

ii) not all of the people surveyed back etiquette

> Secondly, the writer does not claim that everyone surveyed backs etiquette.

(2 marks)

**TOTAL FOR SECTION A = 10 MARKS**

# Sample Reading answers – fail

**7** What it the main purpose of Text B?

Satellite navigation systems ............................................

> This is incorrect because it does not say why the text was written (its purpose).

(1 mark)

**8** Give **three** features of Text B that help to convey information.

You do **not** need to write in sentences.

i) easy understanding to make you aware

> This is incorrect because it does not explain how it is easy to understand (e.g. by the question and answer format).

ii) Where should my satnav be fitted

> This is incorrect because it does not explain how this helps to convey information (e.g. it is a sub-heading showing what the section is about, and it is written in bold so that it stands out).

iii) Don't put it near an airbag

> This is incorrect because it is the information conveyed rather than a feature that helps to convey information.

(3 marks)

**9** Apart from your satnav, give two examples from Text B of what you must take into consideration when driving safely.

You do **not** need to write in sentences.

i) fix away from the airbag covers

> This is incorrect because it is about a satnav. The question asks for considerations apart from your satnav.

ii) what you must do if something goes wrong

> This is incorrect because it is unclear and not an example from Text B.

(2 marks)

# Sample Reading answers – fail

This is incorrect because this advice is given in the section about where the satnav should be fitted rather than what to do to change destination location.

**10** According to Text B, what should you do if you want to enter information into your satnav?

Read the instructions for the satnav device

(1 mark)

**11** Your friend is considering buying a satnav. Which **three** aspects from Text B do you think are the most important for them to understand?

You do **not** need to write in sentences.

i) Obey road signs, road works

This is incorrect because it is not relevant to buying a satnav.

ii) Easy to use

This is incorrect because Text B does not say that a satnav is easy to use.

iii) Safety of information

This is incorrect because it is unclear.

(3 marks)

_____

**TOTAL FOR SECTION B = 10 MARKS**

# Sample Reading answers – fail

**12** Your friend is looking for a car with a manual gearbox and has a budget of £500. Which of the three cars in Text C would you recommend?

Remember to give the number of the advert in your answer.

You do **not** need to write in sentences.

Car in Advert 1 ..............................................................................................

> This is incorrect because although this car has a manual gearbox it costs £599 and is therefore too expensive for your friend.

(1 mark)

**13** A member of your family would also like a car. She would like a car with good safety features. Which of the three cars in Text C would you recommend?

Remember to give the number of the advert in your answer.

You do **not** need to write in sentences.

Car in Advert 2 ..............................................................................................

> This is incorrect because this advert does not mention any safety features.

(1 mark)

**14** Consider the information provided in the three adverts in Text C. Based on this information which car would you choose to go and look at?

Give **three** reasons.

Remember to give the number of the advert in your answer.

You do **not** need to write in sentences.

Car chosen    Car in Advert 1 because it had 3 previous owners. This shows that it is good.

Reason i)    Car in Advert 2 because it has done 83,000 miles.

Reason ii)    Car in Advert 3 because it is currently untaxed.

Reason iii)    ..............................................................................................

> This is incorrect because the conclusion does not follow – it shows that 3 previous owners have decided to sell the car.

> This is incorrect because it is not a valid reason to choose this car over the other two which have both done fewer miles.

> This is not a valid reason to choose this car because it means you would have to pay road tax charges on top of the cost of the car.

(3 marks)

**TOTAL FOR SECTION C = 5 MARKS**

**TOTAL FOR PAPER = 25 MARKS**

# Sample Writing answers – pass

There are **two** tasks which assess your writing skills.

Remember that spelling, punctuation and grammar will be assessed in **both** tasks.

**Task 1**

**Information**

Your school/college/workplace has asked for ideas about a charitable project to support. You have found this information about mobile phone recycling.

**The Phone Shop Mobile Phone Recycling Scheme**

**Recycle your phone – to help the environment and to help local charities.**

Recycling is easy to do, great for the environment and won't cost you a penny.

The Phone Shop has teamed up with Charitable Mobile Recycling (CMR) to launch a simple scheme that raises money for charity from unwanted mobile phones. This also prevents mobile phones going to landfill sites. For every 200 phones recycled we will donate £300 to local charities.

**Mobile phone facts**
- The average mobile phone user will replace their handset once every 18 months.
- Less than 20% of all unused mobile phones in the UK are currently recycled.
- Latest figures suggest close to 90 million phones are never used. If you put 90 million phones end to end, they would stretch from Lands End to John O'Groats and back OVER THREE TIMES.
- Mobile phones contain toxic substances which need to be disposed of in a safe manner. If these end up in landfill sites they become a threat to human health and the environment.

**How do I recycle my mobile phone?**

First you need to register for the scheme at our website www.thephoneshop/Recycling

Collection boxes are available if you are collecting 20 phones or more. Just order a collection box when you register and when it is full arrange a FREE collection through our website. This is ideal for an office, college or school collection.

You can recycle mobile phones of any brand and in any condition. Every phone can make a difference.

**Writing task**

Write a briefing paper about this scheme to help your school/college/workplace make its decision.

In your briefing paper, you may include:
- background information about the scheme
- the advantages and disadvantages of running this scheme at your school/college/workplace
- whether or not you recommend this scheme.

(15 marks)

# Sample Writing answers – pass

This scheme I have found will benefit the environment, each year thousands of people throw away their unwanted mobile phones. These phones contain a chemical substance which can harm both the human population and the environment. The Phone Shop has teamed up with the Charitable Mobile Recycling to launch a scheme to raise money for local charities from donated mobiles.

The advantages of this scheme if you choose to participate is that we will be doing a great deal to others, the money raised can be used to help or set up new youth clubs which can then keep young children/adults off the streets, and in a safe location.

Of course there will be some disadvantages for this scheme such as: not everyone will donate a phone either because they just don't want to or they don't possess a mobile phone. Even if the charity does invest into a youth club, not everyone will want to go, so there will still be gang members and drug dealers on the streets. 200 phones are quite a lot, especially for £300 back.

**A: Form, communication and purpose = 6 marks**

**B: Spelling, punctuation and grammar = 5 marks**

**Total = 11/15 (see next page for examiner's comments)**

**TOTAL FOR TASK 1 = 15 MARKS**

# Sample Writing answers – pass

| What has been done well | |
|---|---|
| Clear concise description of the aims of the scheme | Explains who is running the scheme, and that it involves donations of unwanted mobile phones to benefit the environment and raise money for charity |
| Identifies some general advantages and disadvantages of the scheme | Explains how the money could be spent, some of the difficulties of collecting enough phones and the limitations of the youth club idea |
| Uses appropriate tone for the purpose | Maintains formal tone |
| Paragraphing | New paragraphs for each section; background to the scheme; advantages and disadvantages |
| Able to construct complex sentences | E.g. 'Even if the charity does invest into a youth club, not everyone will want to go, so ... |
| Accurate spelling | No errors |
| Can use apostrophes correctly | E.g. use of apostrophe in "don't" |
| **What could be improved** | |
| Include a heading | To indicate what the briefing paper is about |
| Provide an introduction | To give the context |
| Describe how the scheme works in more detail | So that the reader can assess whether the scheme will work |
| Explain the advantages and disadvantages for your school/college/workplace | E.g. easy to operate, free collection, many people can be involved, every phone makes a difference; but site for collection box would need to be convenient and secure, someone needs to organise |
| Separate sentences correctly | E.g. in the first line, the comma should be a full stop |
| Provide a recommendation | To sum up and provide clear guidance |

# Sample Writing answers – strong pass

A response to your request for ideas about a charitable project for the school to support.
I would like to inform you about the Phone Shop Mobile Phone Recycling Scheme.

This scheme is run jointly by The Phone Shop and Charitable Mobile Recycling (CMR) and aims to raise money for charity from unwanted mobile phones.
- For every 200 phones donated to The Phone Shop, CMR gives £300 for local charities.
- The phones can be of any brand and in any condition.

There are many advantages to this scheme:
- Recycling mobile phones is great for the environment
- Mobile phones contain toxic substances which need to be disposed of safely rather than ending up in landfill sites where they are a threat to our health and the environment
- It is an easy way to help local charities. According to statistics from The Phone Shop, on average people replace their mobile phones every 18 months, and there are 90 million phones that are never used.

So, there must be a lot of phones which could be recycled; less than 20% of mobile phones in the UK are currently recycled.

The scheme would be good for the school because:
- It would cost nothing to operate and would be good publicity if we can raise lots of money for charity
- We have a lot of pupils in the school and most of them have mobiles, and teachers and parents could also be asked for their old phones
- Everyone can take part so it would be good for community spirit and people will have somewhere to get rid of their unwanted phones.

The only disadvantages are that you have to have a convenient place where the phones can be collected and it might take quite a long time to collect 200 phones. However, they will give you a collection box for free if you are collecting 20 phones or more and they will collect the box when it is full.

I think this is a really good scheme for the school to take part in because it benefits everybody. As they say, "Recycling is easy to do, great for the environment and won't cost you a penny."

If you decide to register for the scheme, they have a website, www.thephoneshop/Recycling.

**A: Form, communication and purpose = 9 marks**

**B: Spelling, punctuation and grammar = 6 marks**

**Total = 15/15 (see next page for examiner's comments)**

**TOTAL FOR TASK 1 = 15 MARKS**

# Sample Writing answers – strong pass

| What has been done well | |
|---|---|
| Includes an appropriate heading | Gives title of scheme |
| Clear introduction | Gives the context |
| Concise but detailed description of the scheme | Explains who is running the scheme, why and how it works |
| Detailed explanation of advantages of the scheme | Explains benefits for the environment, local charities, the school and individuals |
| Clear sense of audience and purpose | E.g. ' A response to your request …' |
| Good organisation | Effective use of headings, bullets and paragraphs, use of connective e.g. 'However..' |
| Accurate use of sentence structures | Uses a range of sentence structures to present complex ideas |
| Accurate spelling | No errors |
| Accurate use of punctuation | Commas, apostrophes, quotation marks |
| Grammatically correct | Subject-verb agreement, use of tenses |
| **What could be improved** | |
| More detailed discussion of disadvantages for the school | E.g. Security of collection site, organisation issues, etc |
| More developed recommendation | To emphasise benefits |

# Sample Writing answers – fail

Hello ladies and Gentlemen. Today I'm going to tell you why we as a school should chosse "The Mobile Phone Recycling Scheme".

The mobile phone recycling Scheme is a good way of giving money to a charity. everyone has new phones so what do you do with the old one? Throw it away, why do that when you can give it to someone who needs a phone.

The good things are for every 200 phone we donate they get a £300 and since there is over 1000 kids in this school and over 200 teachers they will be getting loads of money. And since it's a fact people renew there phone every 18 months. Also I bet you didn't know this mobile phones carry a toxic substance which needs to be disposed in a safe manner.

me myself recommend this scheme I hope you do to.

Thank you for your time.

**A: Form, communication and purpose = 5 marks**

**B: Spelling, punctuation and grammar = 3 marks**

**Total = 8/13 (see next page for examiner's comments)**

**TOTAL FOR TASK 1 = 15 MARKS**

# Sample Writing answers – fail

| What has been done well | |
|---|---|
| Clear description of scheme and some of its advantages | Name of scheme, £300 for 200 phones, need for safe disposal of toxic substances |
| Lively expression of ideas | Use of rhetorical, 'I bet you didn't know … ' |
| Clear recommendation | using complex sentences |
| Some organisation of information | Effective paragraphing |
| Reasonably accurate spelling | Only three errors, 'chosse' (choose), 'there' (their), 'to' (too) |
| Quotation marks used correctly | for title of scheme |
| **What could be improved** | |
| Clearer explanation of how the scheme would benefit the school | E.g. most people could be involved, helping to build community spirit. |
| Some consideration of possible disadvantages | E.g. may be difficult to persuade people to donate old mobiles, might take time to see benefits. |
| Explain the recommendation | Say why the advantages outweigh the disadvantages. |
| Provide a heading | To show what the briefing paper is about. |
| Use a more business-like tone | Introduction seems more suitable for an advertising pitch. |
| Significant errors in grammar and punctuation | Incorrect or missing punctuation affecting the sense of the writing, incorrect subject-verb agreement, incomplete sentences, not starting a sentence with a capital letter, inconsistent use of capital letters. |

# Sample Writing answers – pass

**Task 2**

**Information**

You live in Rook Lane and have received this information sheet.

## Estrick County Council Notice to Residents

## Access arrangements for forthcoming Fun Fair

The fun fair is coming to Estrick Park in the centre of the town from July 7th–July 11th.

Cycle paths across the park will be closed during this period.

Car parking for visitors will be made available in the following roads: Banks Lane, Douglas Street, Chandlers Road and Market Street.

Temporary toilets will be placed in Rook Lane. Rook Lane will be closed to traffic. Residents should make alternative arrangements for parking.

If you wish to comment on any of these arrangements, please contact Cathy Oldman at Estrick County Council.

Email: c.oldman@estrickcc.gov.uk

**Writing task**

You are very unhappy about the arrangements for the fun fair.

Write an email to Cathy Oldman at Estrick County Council, protesting against the arrangements.

(10 marks)

**Begin your answer on the next page.**

# Sample Writing answers – pass

| New Message |
| --- |
| **From:** you@your.email.co.uk |
| **To:** c.oldman@estrickcc.gov.uk |
| **Subject:** Fun Fair arrangements |

Dear Miss C Oldman

I am very unhappy about these arrangements that have been made for this fun fair. The area I live in is always packed of cars, we sometimes don't even get space to park our cars. You have closed Rook Lane for traffic and told us to make other arrangements. Also you have choosen to put the toilets on my road, which I am not happy about. My children play on the road very often and I don't want them near the toilets. It will also leave a very bad smell for the residents of my road.

Please could you make other arrangements for your fair as the ones made are very inconvenient.

Yours sincerly

**A: Form, communication and purpose = 4 marks**

**B: Spelling, punctuation and grammar = 3 marks**

**Total – 7/10 (see next page for examiner's comments)**

**TOTAL FOR TASK 2 = 10 MARKS**

**TOTAL FOR PAPER = 25 MARKS**

# Sample Writing answers – pass

| What has been done well | |
|---|---|
| Clear explanation of complaint | Difficult to park, position of toilets where children play, smell for residents. |
| Polite, business-like tone | No use of slang or colloquial language, not aggressive |
| Correct format | The greeting is appropriate and matches the close. |
| Some limited use of paragraphs | New paragraph for the brief conclusion |
| Reasonable technical accuracy | Only two spelling mistakes (choosen, sincerly), generally accurate grammar and punctuation. |
| **What could be improved** | |
| Explain the negative effects of the fun fair arrangements in more detail | E.g. danger to health and safety, loss of trade, stress and inconvenience to residents, etc. |
| Suggest alternative arrangements or request more specific action | E.g. somewhere else to park, place the toilets, hold the fun fair |
| Vary sentence structure | Use connectives other than 'and' to show how sentences relate to each other; e.g 'The area I live in is always packed of (with) cars, so we sometimes don't even get space to park our cars.' |

# Sample Writing answers – fail

**Task 2**

**Information**

You live in Rook Lane and have received this information sheet.

## Estrick County Council Notice to Residents

## Access arrangements for forthcoming Fun Fair

The fun fair is coming to Estrick Park in the centre of the town from July 7th–July 11th.

Cycle paths across the park will be closed during this period.

Car parking for visitors will be made available in the following roads: Banks Lane, Douglas Street, Chandlers Road and Market Street.

Temporary toilets will be placed in Rook Lane. Rook Lane will be closed to traffic. Residents should make alternative arrangements for parking.

If you wish to comment on any of these arrangements, please contact Cathy Oldman at Estrick County Council.

Email: c.oldman@estrickcc.gov.uk

**Writing task**

You are very unhappy about the arrangements for the fun fair.

Write an email to Cathy Oldman at Estrick County Council, protesting against the arrangements.

(10 marks)

**Begin your answer on the next page.**

# Sample Writing answers – fail

| New Message |
| --- |
| **From:** you@your.email.co.uk |
| **To:** c.oldman@estrickcc.gov.uk |
| **Subject:** Fun Fair arrangements |

Dear Mrs Cathy Oldman,

I am writing to you, to say that I am very unhappy. Its the fact that the fun fair will be open but the path wouldn't, so that makes me and the other cyclist on the road? I am very unhappy that I have to put myself indanger on the road. If i be in an accident I will report to you especially. It isnt fair to all of us.

Temporary toilets will not be permitted because it will cause polution, I dont think you have thought about it. And for people to park on the roads can cause accidents.

There are aloud of things that I could of said. It needs to be sorted and I am going to be talking to the council.

**A: Form, communication and purpose = 2 marks**

**B: Spelling, punctuation and grammar = 2 marks**

**Total – 4/10 (see next page for examiner's comments)**

**TOTAL FOR TASK 2 = 10 MARKS**

**TOTAL FOR PAPER = 25 MARKS**

# Sample Writing answers – fail

| What has been done well | |
|---|---|
| Some attempt to organise ideas | Use of paragraphs |
| Some elements of correct format for a formal email | Appropriate greeting |
| Reasonably accurate spelling | Few mistakes: 'indanger' should be two words, 'polution' (pollution), 'aloud' (a load), 'of' (have) **but** accident, permitted, temporary all correct. |
| **What could be improved** | |
| Make sure the sense is clear | E.g. why is the second sentence a question? Cathy Oldman works for the council so what is meant by the final sentence? |
| State clearly what you expect to be done | 'It needs to be sorted' is very vague. |
| Close the email correctly | 'Yours sincerely' would match the greeting used |
| Check punctuation | Incorrect use of question mark and commas, apostrophes left out. |
| Check grammar | Use of wrong tense in 'the fun fair will be open but the path wouldn't' and 'If i be in an accident' |

# Reading practice assessment

Read Text A and answer questions 1–6.

**Text A**

You are looking for unusual gift ideas and have found this information on the Internet.

## Gift Ideas to Avoid

Yes, there **can be** such a thing as a **bad gift** ...

However, there's no need to panic, the **Big Fat Balloons School of Gift Buying** is here to help. So you don't have to make amends with our **Sorry Balloon in a Box** (pictured left) we've compiled **a list of gift ideas to avoid**.

### Appliances as romantic gifts

**Never, ever give an appliance to your wife or girlfriend as a gift.**

Unless you are certain she dreams of owning a deluxe mixer because cooking is her passion – **stay clear from appliances**. Especially avoid vacuum cleaners, washing machines or any other device that might be used to clean up after you.

### Gifts that are too generic or too cheap

Mugs, toiletries and lottery tickets are often given as presents. Although they might be suitable for people you don't know very well, beware when buying these for close friends and family. This kind of gift just says: '*I really had no idea... so here you are.*'

You also need to make sure the **value of the gift matches the occasion**. I once spoke to a man who remembered his disappointment when receiving a shirt from his girlfriend on his 40th birthday... He was expecting a more memorable – and more personal – gift for that special occasion (he now has a new girlfriend).

### Clothes

Clothes are usually **best avoided**, unless you have seen the recipient try it on and put it back because they could not afford it. Chances are that you will get the **style, size or colour wrong**.

However clothes **can make great gifts if you get it right**. Some might even consider using gift giving to curb an addiction to unflattering clothing or bad taste... think of it as clothes rehab through gifts... However, tread carefully and make sure your own taste is impeccable and you know the recipient well. If in doubt stick to clothes vouchers!

**1** What is the main purpose of Text A?

.................................................................................................................

(1 mark)

**Answer questions 2 to 3 with a cross in the box ⊠. If you change your mind about an answer, put a line through the box ⊠ and then mark your new answer with a cross ⊠.**

**2** According to Text A, a lottery ticket is a suitable gift to give:

A ☐ your wife or girlfriend

B ☐ a close friend

C ☐ for a special occasion

D ☐ an acquaintance

(1 mark)

**3** Text A advises against buying clothes as a present because:

A ☐ clothing is very personal

B ☐ clothes are too expensive

C ☐ it is easier to give a voucher

D ☐ some people have bad taste

(1 mark)

**4** Identify **two** reasons why the person receiving a gift might be disappointed, according to Text A. You do **not** need to write in sentences.

i) .........................................................................................................

.........................................................................................................

ii) .........................................................................................................

.........................................................................................................

(2 marks)

**5** Place a tick in the correct column for **each** of the six statements to show which are presented in the article as facts and which are opinions.

|  | Fact | Opinion |
|---|---|---|
| Toiletries are often given as presents. | | |
| Buying a mug as a gift shows lack of thought. | | |
| It is difficult to buy the right clothes for someone else. | | |
| A vacuum cleaner is an electrical appliance. | | |
| An appliance is unsuitable as a romantic gift. | | |
| A 40th birthday is regarded as a special occasion. | | |

(3 marks)

**6** Text A claims it wants to help readers avoid buying bad gifts.

From your reading of the information provided, give **two** reasons why this text might be biased.

You do **not** need to write in sentences.

i) ................................................................................................................................

................................................................................................................................

ii) ...............................................................................................................................

................................................................................................................................

(2 marks)

---

**TOTAL FOR SECTION A = 10 MARKS**

**SECTION B**

Read Text B and answer questions 7–11.

**Text B**

# Gifts – Your Rights

When buying a new present from a trader, you have all the normal rights under the Sale Of Goods Act 1979 (amended).

**Remember, goods must be:**

- of satisfactory quality; so they should be fit for their usual purposes, safe, reasonably durable, free from faults, of satisfactory appearance and generally what a reasonable person would expect
- as described verbally by the seller, in adverts and displays, on outer packaging
- Fit for any particular purpose that you made known to the seller, for example a watch suitable for scuba diving.

**Who can enforce these rights?**

If you tell the seller that the item is to be a present, then the seller can, at the time of sale, insist on dealing only with you, the purchaser. This rarely happens, and indeed some retailers actually give gift receipts for the recipient to use to prove the contract. Therefore the recipient of the gift can usually deal with any faulty goods.

These rights cover any gift or item bought by one person for another, but make sure that the seller is aware of when the gift is due to be given.

**What if I still have problems?**

If you have any problems or questions about presents – or any goods or services – more information is available from the Consumer Direct website. They can be contacted by phone on 09054 040506.

**7** What is the main purpose of Text B?

.......................................................................................................................................................

(1 mark)

**8** Give **three** features of Text B that help to convey information.

You do **not** need to write in sentences.

i) ..........................................................................................................................................

..........................................................................................................................................

ii) ..........................................................................................................................................

..........................................................................................................................................

iii) ..........................................................................................................................................

..........................................................................................................................................

(3 marks)

**9** Identify **two** reasons why you could complain to a trader about something you bought from them, according to Text B.

You do **not** need to write in sentences.

i) ..........................................................................................................................................

..........................................................................................................................................

ii) ..........................................................................................................................................

..........................................................................................................................................

(2 marks)

**10** According to Text B, how can you obtain further assistance if things go wrong?

You do **not** need to write in sentences.

.......................................................................................................................................................

.......................................................................................................................................................

(1 mark)

**11** Your friend is planning to buy a gift for someone. Using the information from Text B, describe **three** pieces of advice on dealing with the seller you would give your friend to help protect their legal rights.

You do **not** need to write in sentences.

i) ...........................................................................................................................................

...........................................................................................................................................

ii) ..........................................................................................................................................

...........................................................................................................................................

iii) .........................................................................................................................................

...........................................................................................................................................

(3 marks)

**TOTAL FOR SECTION B = 10 MARKS**

**SECTION C**

Read Text C and answer questions 12–14.

**Text C**

You have found some information on experiences that can be given as gifts.

## Paintball Pass for 8  (Experience 1)

**Experience Summary:** Up to eight places on a full day paintball experience. All equipment except paint included. Paintballs can be purchased on the day.

**Availability:** Start time is usually around 09:30. Allow for spending all day at the venue.

**Requirements:** Minimum age 12 years. You must be in reasonable health and be fairly fit to take part. You should wear sturdy footwear, suitable for a woodland environment, and loose comfortable clothing.

## Horse Drawn Carriage Country Pub Run (Experience 2)

**Experience Summary:** You may be part of a group of up to 12 people. Your journey will take you through the country lanes leading to the local pub, where you will be served with lunch. Highly experienced staff can share their knowledge of the horses before your return journey to the farm.

**Availability:** Carriages leave from the farm at midday. The experience lasts for approximately 2½ hours.

**Requirements:** No minimum age. Children must be accompanied by a participating adult.

## Gorge Walking  (Experience 3)

**Experience Summary:** There are two gorges to choose from: the first, particularly suitable for family groups, includes scrambling and jumps or mud slides into plunge pools; the second is more challenging and involves rope work as you are lowered over rocks and down waterfalls. Fully qualified instructors will provide a safety briefing.

**Availability:** Walks operate as half-day sessions lasting around three hours. Typical start times are 09:30 and 13:30.

**Requirements:** The minimum age is eight; there is no upper age limit. You do not have to know how to swim, but you need to be confident in water. All equipment is provided. You will need a t-shirt and swimsuit to wear under your wetsuit, and shoes that you don't mind getting wet.

**12** You have a relative with very young children. Which of the three experiences in Text C would be most suitable as a gift?

Remember to give the number of the experience in your answer.

You do **not** need to write in sentences.

...................................................................................................................................................

(1 mark)

**13** A teenage friend is very fit and loves physical activities but finds it difficult to get up early. Which of the three experiences in Text C would be most suitable?

Remember to give the number of the experience in your answer.

You do **not** need to write in sentences.

...................................................................................................................................................

(1 mark)

**14** Consider the information provided in the description of the three experiences in Text C. Based on this information, which experience would you most like to be given?

Give **three** reasons.

Remember to give the number of the experience in your answer.

You do **not** need to write in sentences.

Experience chosen .............................................................................................................

Reason i) ...........................................................................................................................

Reason ii) ..........................................................................................................................

Reason iii) .........................................................................................................................

(3 marks)

---

**TOTAL FOR SECTION C = 5 MARKS**

**TOTAL FOR PAPER = 25 MARKS**

# Mark scheme: Reading

## Reading Level 2 practice assessment answers

### Section A

| Question Number | Answer | Mark |
| --- | --- | --- |
| 1 | To warn the reader why certain types of gifts might be unsuitable (1)<br><br>Accept any reasonable answer based on the text. | (1) |

| Question Number | Answer | Mark |
| --- | --- | --- |
| 2 | D – an acquaintance | (1) |

| Question Number | Answer | Mark |
| --- | --- | --- |
| 3 | A – clothing is very personal | (1) |

| Question Number | Answer | Mark |
| --- | --- | --- |
| 4 | • too ordinary/does not show enough thought (1)<br>• too impersonal (1)<br>• value does not match the occasion (1)<br><br>One mark for each correct answer, up to a maximum of **two** marks | (2) |

| Question Number | Answer | Mark |
| --- | --- | --- |
| 5 | | |

|  | Fact | Opinion |
| --- | --- | --- |
| Toiletries are often given as presents. | ✓ | |
| Buying a mug as a gift shows lack of thought. | | ✓ |
| It is difficult to buy the right clothes for someone else. | | ✓ |
| A vacuum cleaner is an electrical appliance. | ✓ | |
| An appliance is unsuitable as a romantic gift. | | ✓ |
| A 40th birthday is regarded as a special occasion. | ✓ | |

**For 0 or 1 correct – 0 marks**
**For 2 or 3 correct - 1 mark**
**For 4 or 5 correct – 2 marks**
**For 6 correct – 3 marks** (3)

| Question Number | Answer | Mark |
| --- | --- | --- |
| 6 | Answers may include:<br>• vested interest/written by an organisation selling gifts of their own/includes links to own products (1)<br>• limited/only anecdotal supporting evidence ('I once spoke to a man…')(1)<br>• persuasive language e.g. 'never, ever …', 'avoid', 'stay clear'<br>• exaggeration (addiction to unflattering clothing) for humorous effect. (1)<br><br>Accept any reasonable answer, based on the text, up to a maximum of **two** marks. | (2) |

## Section B

| Question Number | Answer | Mark |
|---|---|---|
| 7 | To inform the reader of their rights when buying a present.<br><br>Accept any reasonable answer based on the text. | (1) |

| Question Number | Answer | Mark |
|---|---|---|
| 8 | Answers may include:<br>• question and answer style make the information clear (1)<br>• use of bold makes title/headings stand out/easy to locate (1)<br>• use of bold for emphasis (1)<br>• bullet point list of descriptors of satisfactory criteria (1)<br>• use of image representing faulty goods (1)<br>• weblink to indicate further information available. (1)<br><br>Accept any reasonable answer, based on the text, up to a maximum of **three** marks. | (3) |

| Question Number | Answer | Mark |
|---|---|---|
| 9 | • goods are faulty (unfit for usual purpose/unsafe/not working)<br>• appearance of goods is unsatisfactory<br>• goods are not as described<br>• goods cannot be used for a specific purpose, previously agreed with seller<br><br>One mark for each correct answer up to a maximum of **two**. | (2) |

| Question Number | Answer | Mark |
|---|---|---|
| 10 | Contact Consumer Direct by phone or internet  (1) | (1) |

| Question Number | Answer | Mark |
|---|---|---|
| 11 | Answers may include:<br>• tell the seller if the goods will be a gift (1)<br>• ask for a gift receipt (1)<br>• tell the seller when the gift will be given (1)<br>• explain to the seller any special purpose the gift will be used for (1)<br>• check the quality and appearance of the goods. (1)<br><br>Accept any reasonable answer, based on the text, up to a maximum of **three** marks. | (3) |

| Question Number | Answer | Mark |
|---|---|---|
| 12 | Experience 2 | (1) |

| Question Number | Answer | Mark |
|---|---|---|
| 13 | Experience 3 | (1) |

| Question Number | Answer | Mark |
|---|---|---|
| 15 | Any experience may be chosen. Reasons may include:<br>• type of activity<br>• duration<br>• preference for solo/group activity<br>• previous experience<br>• health/fitness<br>• confidence in water<br>• possible extra costs.<br>Award one mark for each reason, up to a maximum of **three** marks. | (3) |

# Mapping to Functional Skills Criteria for English Level 2

**Reading**

| Question | Fixed Marks | Open Marks | Mapping to standard — Select, read, understand and compare texts and use them to gather information, ideas, arguments and opinions. | | | | |
|---|---|---|---|---|---|---|---|
| | | | (L2.2.1) Select and use different types of texts to obtain and utilise relevant information | (L2.2.2) Read and summarise, succinctly, information / ideas from different sources | (L2.2.3) Identify the purposes of texts and comment on how meaning is conveyed | (L2.2.4) Detect point of view, implicit meaning and/or bias | (L2.2.5) Analyse texts in relation to audience needs and consider suitable responses |
| 1 | | 1 | | | ✓ | | |
| 2 | 1 | | ✓ | | | | |
| 3 | 1 | | ✓ | | | | |
| 4 | 2 | | | ✓ | | | |
| 5 | 3 | | | | | ✓ | |
| 6 | | 2 | | | | ✓ | |
| 7 | | 1 | | | ✓ | | |
| 8 | | 3 | | | ✓ | | |
| 9 | 2 | | ✓ | | | | |
| 10 | 1 | | ✓ | | | | |
| 11 | | 3 | | | | | ✓ |
| 12 | 1 | | | | | | ✓ |
| 13 | 1 | | | | | | ✓ |
| 14 | | 3 | | ✓ | | | |
| **Total marks:** | | | 5 | 5 | 5 | 5 | 5 |
| **Total percentage:** | | | 20 | 20 | 20 | 20 | 20 |

# Writing practice assessment

There are **two** tasks which assess your writing skills. Task 1 is worth 15 marks and Task 2 is worth 10 marks.

Remember that spelling, punctuation and grammar will be assessed in **both** tasks.

You may use a dictionary.

**Task 1**

**Information**

Your school or college has asked for ideas about where to hold a leaving party for students who are about to complete their studies. You have found this information about a local venue within your budget.

## Facilities for Celebrations & Conferences

**The Elms Country Hotel**
Built approximately 300 years ago, The Elms Country Hotel offers modern facilities whilst maintaining the traditional character of the building. Set in twelve acres of beautiful parkland and gardens, it provides the perfect location for your meeting, conference or party requirement.

| The Conference Suite |
| --- |
| The Conference Suite at The Elms Country Hotel seats 60 persons.<br>Toilet facilities are situated elsewhere in the venue.<br>There is a bar elsewhere in the venue. |
| A full table catering service is available; for other catering options please discuss with the venue. |
| There is parking on-site. |
| The Elms Country Hotel has grounds and gardens suitable for use as a photographic backdrop, e.g. for wedding pictures. There are other photo opportunity options very close by. |

| Room Facilities | | | |
| --- | --- | --- | --- |
| ✓ | Dance floor | ✓ | Sound/PA |
| ✗ | Stage | ✓ | Blackout blinds |
| ✗ | Stage lighting | ✓ | Video projection |
| ✗ | Air conditioning | | |

**Writing task**

Write a briefing paper about this venue to help your school/college make its decision.

In your briefing paper, you may include:

- details of the venue
- the advantages and disadvantages of using this venue for the leaving party e.g. size, location, ease of access, facilities
- whether or not you recommend this venue.

**TOTAL FOR TASK 1 = 15 MARKS**

**Task 2**

**Information**

You have seen this report in your local newspaper.

> # YOUTH CENTRE MAY CLOSE
>
> ## 'Building unsafe and expensive to repair' says Council
>
> A proposal to demolish the council-owned building in Cavendish Road presently occupied by Starlight Youth Centre will be voted on next week by Manordale Council members. This comes in the wake of a report by council engineers claiming that the hundred year old building is unsafe and will cost many thousands of pounds to repair.
>
> Councillor Sally Jemson, who put forward the motion, said: 'We really have to look at what we are spending taxpayers' money on in these difficult economic conditions. I don't think we can justify throwing money away on a facility which is of little value to the community as a whole.'
>
> The future of the Starlight Centre, which provides games and social activities for local teenagers, is uncertain. Youth Organiser Phil Adams commented, "If this proposal goes through, I don't know if we will be able to carry on – there are no other suitable premises in the area we could use instead."

**Writing task**

You feel strongly about whether the building should be demolished and you have decided to write to your local councillor to tell them your views.

Write an email to your local councillor, Councillor Martin Innes, explaining why you do or do not support the proposal to demolish the building.

| New Message |
| --- |
| **From:** you@your.email.co.uk |
| **To:** councillor.martin.innes@manordale.gov.uk |
| **Subject:** Proposal to demolish building in Cavendish Road |

**TOTAL FOR TASK 2 = 10 MARKS**

**TOTAL FOR PAPER = 25 MARKS**

# Mark scheme: Writing

## Writing Level 2 practice assessment

Marks for each task are awarded by applying the two grids below:

**A: Form, communication and purpose**

**B: Spelling, punctuation and grammar.**

Each marking grid, A and B, should be applied independently because you may have a different level of ability under each heading.

| Task | |
|---|---|
| 1 | Write a briefing paper about this venue to help your school/college make its decision. <br><br> In your briefing paper, you may include: <br> • details of the venue <br> • the advantages and disadvantages of using this venue for the leaving party <br> • whether or not you recommend this venue. <br><br> **(15 marks)** |
| | **Indicative content** |
| | • Shows awareness of organisational features of a briefing paper. <br> • Uses appropriate tone/language when writing the briefing paper. <br> • Some detail regarding the content of the briefing paper and its purpose. <br> • Some explanation of the hotel and what it offers as a venue. <br> • The advantages and disadvantages of holding a school/college leaving party in this venue. <br> • Reasons given on whether or not they would recommend the venue. |

| Mark | A: Form, communication and purpose |
|---|---|
| 0 | No rewardable material. |
| 1–3 | • Presents relevant information/ideas logically to a limited extent. <br> • Basic ability to present complex ideas/information evident. <br> • Uses language for specific purpose to a limited extent. <br> • Uses a limited range of sentence structures with limited accuracy. <br> • Makes limited use of paragraphing and other organisational features with basic accuracy. |
| 4–6 | • Presents relevant information/ideas logically for some of the response. <br> • Able to present complex ideas/information clearly and concisely with some lapses. <br> • Uses language for specific purpose for some of the response. <br> • Uses a range of sentence structures with some accuracy. <br> • Makes some use of paragraphing and other organisational features with some accuracy. |
| 7–9 | • Presents relevant information/ideas logically for most of the response. <br> • Able to present complex ideas/information clearly and concisely with occasional lapses. <br> • Uses language for specific purpose throughout the response. <br> • Uses a range of sentence structures with accuracy. <br> • Makes consistent use of paragraphing and other organisational features with accuracy. |

| Mark | B: Spelling, punctuation and grammar |
|------|--------------------------------------|
| 0 | No rewardable material. |
| 1–2 | • Uses spelling and grammar with limited accuracy, supporting meaning at a basic level.<br>• Uses basic punctuation e.g. commas, apostrophes and inverted commas with limited accuracy. |
| 3–4 | • Uses spelling and grammar with some accuracy, supporting meaning for some of the time.<br>• Uses some punctuation e.g. commas, apostrophes and inverted commas correctly and appropriately. |
| 5–6 | • Use of spelling and grammar is mostly accurate, supporting meaning most of the time.<br>• Uses a range of punctuation e.g. commas, apostrophes and inverted commas correctly and appropriately most of the time. |

| Task | | |
|------|---|---|
| 2 | | You feel strongly about whether the building should be demolished and you have decided to write to your local councillor to tell them your views.<br><br>Write an email to your local councillor, Councillor Martin Innes, explaining why you do or do not support the proposal to demolish the building.<br><br>**(10 marks)** |
| | **Indicative content** | |
| | | • Uses appropriate organisational features.<br>• Use appropriate tone/language when communicating opinions in an email.<br>• Shows awareness of audience. |

| Mark | A: Form, communication and purpose |
|------|------------------------------------|
| 0 | No rewardable material. |
| 1–2 | • Presents relevant information/ideas logically, using persuasive language as appropriate, to a limited extent.<br>• Basic ability to present complex ideas/information evident.<br>• Uses language for the specific purpose to a limited extent.<br>• Uses a limited range of sentence structures with limited accuracy.<br>• Makes limited use of paragraphing and other organisational features with basic accuracy. |
| 3–4 | • Presents relevant information/ideas logically, using persuasive language as appropriate, for some of the response.<br>• Able to present complex ideas/information clearly and concisely with some lapses.<br>• Uses language for the specific purpose, for some of the response.<br>• Use a range of sentence structures with some accuracy.<br>• Makes some use of paragraphing and other organisational features with some accuracy. |
| 5–6 | • Presents relevant information/ideas logically, using persuasive language as appropriate, for most of the response.<br>• Able to present complex ideas/information clearly and concisely with occasional lapses.<br>• Uses language for the specific purpose, throughout the response.<br>• Uses a range of sentence structures with accuracy.<br>• Makes consistent use of paragraphing and other organisational features. |

| Mark | B: Spelling, punctuation and grammar |
|---|---|
| 0 | No rewardable material. |
| 1–2 | • Uses spelling and grammar with limited accuracy, supporting meaning at a basic level.<br>• Uses basic punctuation e.g. commas, apostrophes and inverted commas with limited accuracy. |
| 3–4 | • Use of spelling and grammar is mostly accurate, supporting meaning most of the time.<br>• Uses some punctuation e.g. commas, apostrophes and inverted commas correctly and appropriately most of the time. |

# Mapping to Functional Skills Criteria for English Level 2

## Writing

## Skill Standard

Write a range of texts, including extended written documents, communicating information, ideas and opinions, effectively and persuasively.

| Criterion Ref. no. | Coverage | Description | No. of marks | % |
|---|---|---|---|---|
| L2.3.1 | Q1 Q2 | • Present information/ideas concisely, logically, and persuasively. | | |
| L2.3.2 | Q1 Q2 | • Present information on complex subjects clearly and concisely. | 15 | 60 |
| L2.3.3 | Q1 Q2 | • Use a range of writing styles for different purposes. | | |
| L2.3.4 | Q1 Q2 | • Use a range of sentence structures, including complex sentences, and paragraphs to organise written communication effectively. | | |
| L2.3.5 | Q1 Q2 | • Punctuate written text using commas, apostrophes and inverted commas accurately. | 10 | 40 |
| L2.3.6 | Q1 Q2 | • Ensure written work is fit for purpose and audience, with accurate spelling and grammar that support clear meaning in a range of text types. | | |
| | | **Total for Writing** | 25 | 100 |

# Speaking, listening and communication

## Speaking, listening and communication task

Complete both tasks below.

### Discussion task

Your school or college has asked for ideas to improve the induction programme for new students.

In groups, discuss ideas for improving the induction. You should decide on up to three recommendations you could put forward to your school council or tutor/supervisor.

Before the discussion, think back to how you were first introduced to life at your school/college and decide what you personally found helpful and what you think could have been done better. Some ideas to get you started are given below.

'I remember getting lost at first because I didn't know where anything was and I'm no good at reading maps. I would have liked more help finding my way around. '

'It took me a long time to make new friends because I only talked to the people I knew from my old school. We did a few icebreaking activities but I never really got to know anyone new.'

'I was frightened of being bullied by the bigger kids – I know now what to do if that ever happened but it would have helped to know how the school deals with that kind of thing.'

'I liked how we were shown how to find things in the library but I can't remember everything we were told.'

'It was strange having so many new names and faces to remember – it took me ages to learn who everybody was!'

### Presentation task

A volunteer group dealing with issues affecting young people has asked your school to become involved in a project to explore some of these issues.

You have been asked to give a presentation on dealing with peer pressure. In your presentation, you might:
· explain what peer pressure is
· explain ways in which peer pressure can influence behaviour
· explain why peer pressure can be an especially strong influence on teenagers
· explore the good and bad effects of peer pressure
· describe some ways of handling peer pressure
· persuade your audience of the benefits of particular methods of dealing with peer pressure.

# Functional Skills in English Level 2: Speaking, Listening and Communication Assessment Record Sheet

Please complete the following information (a separate sheet for each learner)

| Learner name: | Learner number: | Centre number: |
|---|---|---|

Level 2: make a range of contributions to discussions in a range of contexts, including those that are unfamiliar, and make effective presentations

| Activity: Discussion | Date: |
|---|---|
| Please use the space below to note the context of the activity, how it was organised and any learner preparation/support. | |

| Activity: Presentation | Date: |
|---|---|
| Please use the space below to note the context of the activity, how it was organised and any learner preparation/support. | |

The grids should be applied on a 'best fit' basis. To achieve a Level 2 overall a learner should have met each of the Level 2 standards at least once.

**Discussion activity**

| Just below Level 2 | ✓ | Achieved Level 2 | ✓ |
|---|---|---|---|
| Considers complex information with some understanding and gives relevant, sometimes cogent responses in appropriate language. | | Considers complex information and gives relevant, cogent response in appropriate language. | |
| Makes occasionally significant contributions to discussions, taking a range of roles and helping to move discussion forward some of the time. | | Makes significant contributions to discussions, taking a range of roles and helping to move discussion forward. | |

**Presentation activity**

| Just below Level 2 | ✓ | Achieved Level 2 | ✓ |
|---|---|---|---|
| Presents information and ideas clearly and persuasively to others some of the time. | | Presents information and ideas clearly and persuasively to others. | |
| Adapt contributions to suit audience, purpose and situation some of the time. | | Adapt contributions to suit audience, purpose and situation. | |

Please tick the box if the learner has achieved Level 2:

Centre summative comment:

| Assessor signature: | Date: |
|---|---|